James Robinson Planché

William with the Ring

A Romance in Rhyme

James Robinson Planché

William with the Ring

A Romance in Rhyme

ISBN/EAN: 9783744674157

Printed in Europe, USA, Canada, Australia, Japan

Cover: Foto ©Thomas Meinert / pixelio.de

More available books at **www.hansebooks.com**

WILLIAM WITH THE RING.

WILLIAM WITH THE RING.

A Romance

IN RHYME.

BY

J. R. PLANCHÉ.

AUTHOR OF "RECOLLECTIONS AND REFLECTIONS;"
&c., &c., &c.

" Talk not of wasted affection, affection never was wasted ;
If it enrich not the heart of another, its waters returning
Back to their springs, like the rain, shall fill them full of refreshment
That which the fountain sends forth returns again to the fountain."

LONGFELLOW.

LONDON:
TINSLEY BROTHERS, 18, CATHERINE ST., STRAND.
1873.

LONDON
BRADBURY, EVANS, AND CO., PRINTERS, WHITEFRIARS.

THE principal incidents in this Romance formed, originally, the plot of an Opera I wrote for Mr. Felix Mendelssohn Bartholdy, but which, from circumstances I have recently narrated in my " Recollections," was not composed by him. It is necessary to state thus much, as in the dramatic arrangement Messrs. Chappell and Co. of New Bond Street have an interest in the copyright, and are alone authorised to publish any of the words *with music.* .

J. R. P.

CANTO THE FIRST.

THE BURGESS.

WILLIAM WITH THE RING.

CANTO THE FIRST.

THE BURGESS.

I.

It is a lovely summer day, (¹) *
O'er barren down and sandy bay
The white sea-fog has rolled away
    The freshening breeze before,
And now from out the cloudless sky
The morning sun looks laughingly,
O'er chalky cliff and headland high,
    And that long line of shore
That fades into the distance grey,
From where, around thy cape, Blancz, (²)
    The baffled billows roar.

* See Notes at end of each Canto.

II.

And gaily in the morning beams
St. George's gallant ensign streams
From many a turret tall;
It waves o'er Wissant's harbour deep,
And Sangatte's castle-crowned steep,
And Nieulay's moated wall: (³)
And yonder, far as eye may strain,
Where, dotted with black ships, the main
Seems girt as with an iron chain,
And frets beneath the thrall,
That ensign from a hundred masts,
Over beleaguered Calais casts
The shadow of her fall!

III.

And now, behold, another rise—
Far westward, where the stooping skies
Are mingling with the waters blue,
It flutters like a bird to view,
And swelling with the friendly gale,
Like cloud on cloud, sail after sail
Fast mounting form a column bright,

All gleaming in the golden light!
And now a dark hull heaves in sight,
And, like a greyhound from the slip,
Comes bounding on a mighty ship,
With castled prow and gilded stern,
Whose glories seem the waves to burn.
The rows of shields that grace her side,
Her silken standard floating wide,
Her mainsail broad and topmast high,
One blaze of regal heraldry!
Onward the floating pageant comes,
With blare of trumpets, beat of drums,
And as she nears the anchored fleet,
List to the shouts her course that greet—
Shouts that are echoed loud and long
By thousands to the beach that throng,
And pour to Wissant's harbour down
From out King Edward's " Wooden Town." (')

IV.

" St. George for Merry England!" Hark! Hear ye
    not that cry,
As like a wild swan o'er the wave the vessel dances
    by!

Hurl up your hoods and echo back the shout o'er ocean
    green,
"St. George for Merry England! and welcome to its
    Queen!"
St. George for Merry England! Its valiant Lady
    see,
Who made the Scottish Lion quail before the Leopards
    three. (⁵)
She comes with conquest in her train to mark on
    yonder towers,
The same bright banner floating above the Lily
    flowers!
Up, up, my mates, and echo back the shout o'er ocean
    green,
"St. George for Merry England! and welcome to its
    Queen!"

v.

In his scarlet robes the King
Sat 'mid his barons, banquetting.
Ere his ears those sounds had caught,
A breathless page the tidings brought.
Up he started to his feet,
"Haste we sirs, the Queen to greet."

Down the golden goblets went,
Forth they sallied from the tent,
Who shall call that roll of fame?
Who shall count the knights of name,
Round their monarch then who prest,
In warlike steel or peaceful vest,
As through the " Ville de Bois " he rode,
'Mid eager crowds that seaward flowed,
And scarce would yield a passage free,
E'en for that noble company?

VI.

Beside him rode his darling son,
His gallant course but just begun;
Of sable velvet his jupon,
With silver feathers graced,
All else, from chaperon to shoe,
Was of the same funereal hue,
Save gilded spur of knighthood new.
And as on coal-black jennet too
Along the shore he paced,
Each sun-burnt girl of Picardy
Would closer still to press endeavour,

Whilst men, their bonnets waved on high
And shouted, " The Black Prince for ever ! " (⁶)

VII.

Next, the stout Earl of Derby near,
Rode Oxford's valiant John de Vere.
Richard Fitz-Alan—nobler Peer
Hath England never seen—
And side by side the Bohuns twain,
From head to heel in Milan chain
Well armed were they I ween.
And after them, in rich array,
Beauchamp and Burghersh, Seymour, Gray,
Clifford, and Cobham, Talbot, Saye,
Basset, and Chandos.—Well had they
Their vows of knighthood kept.
Witness De Poix, thy daughters fair,
Who but for that chivalrous pair
Had foul dishonour wept.—(⁷)
Stafford, and Multon, Roos, De Lisle—
All leaders famed afar.
Neville, and Audley, void of guile,
And dauntless De la Warr !
Nor must I pass with mention light,

Of chivalry that mirror bright,
Soul of each high emprise,
So justly called "The Gentle Knight,"
Sir Walter Manny, brave in fight
As in the council wise.

VIII.

Oh! 'twas a gallant, glittering train
That spurred across that sandy plain.
Some armed in mail, and some in plate,
Some clad in gorgeous robes of state,
Well furred with gris and gros.
Some in court-pye or coat hardie
Or doublet of pourpointerie,
And single plumed chapeau,
Or cyclas quaint of cendal fair,
Or cloth of gold, or silver rare,
Or flowing houpeland lined with vair,
And broidered belt and gipciere,
And hose of colours twain.
And piked shoon, and trailing sleeves
All slittered into flowers and leaves.
O'er which the grave historian grieves,
And points to statutes vain. (*)

IX.

"The Queen is landing! Back, ye knaves!
Fall back!—What hoa, there!—Ply your staves,
Ye varlets! cleave the press, I say!
Make for the royal train a way!"
Thus cry the marshals of the camp,
As nearer sounds the measured tramp
Of men-at-arms, and the hoarse roar
Of welcome, shakes the startled shore.
And in the distance lances gleam,
And pennons dance and banners stream,
And the shrill clarion's flourish loud
Rings through the clamour of the crowd—
One moment more—to Edward's breast
His beauteous Philippa is prest.

X.

"Welcome, sweet wife! my conquering Queen!
England may well be proud, I ween,
Of her fair champion! So! thou'st taught
The Scots a lesson? Hah! They thought
Because her King was o'er the deep,
An easy harvest they might reap;

Nor deemed the border thou could'st keep.
Now, by my halidome!
Our farmers' wenches next shall meet
These knaves, and with their spindles beat
The red-shanked robbers home!
Welcome, fair Ladies all! Sure we
Both vain and happy men should be,
When such a bevy of beauties rare
Over the sea hath deigned to fare
Our hearts to cheer, our toils to share!
And in good time ye come
To see our flag o'er Calais wave,
And crown, as beauty should, the brave."

XI.

Up spake the Prince of Wales. "For one,
I would some feat of arms were done
Worthy the bold hearts here to do,
Worthy the bright eyes here to view.
How say you, Sire? On Sangatte's hill
Philip of France is lingering still. (⁹)
Let us against him ride!"
"Not so, fair son." And yet a smile
Passed o'er the father's cheek the while—

A smile of joy and pride.
" Already we twelve moons and more
Have lain this stubborn town before;
And now that scarce as many hours
May pass, ere o'er its humbled towers
Shall float our banner wide,
Shall we the risk of losing run
The hard-earned prize so nearly won?
No; let King Philip stay
Until he see that banner wave
O'er those he came too late to save.
Then if he still remain so brave,
Sweet Ned, again we'll play
The game of Cressy o'er, and thou
Shalt gild thy well-won spurs enow
With the best blood that France, I trow,
Hath left to pour away."

XII.

A stir amid that knightly throng,
By archers almost borne along,
A gaunt and ghastly form is seen,
A spectre it might well have been,
So wan, so wasted, was its mien.

So thin, the fingers prest
Against the blood-stained haqueton,
Through which, the sandy soil upon,
The crimson drops fell one by one,
From hurt but rudely drest;
Yet faint and feeble, wounded, worn,
A withering glance of hate and scorn
On the gay crowd he cast.
Then gathered up his dragging chain
As lady fair might do her train;
And with a smile of proud disdain
The English knights he passed.

XIII.

The captain of that archer troop
Kneels at King Edward's feet.
" Now, welcome, good Sir Richard Scroop,
What tidings from our fleet?"
" A vessel, Sire, which, veiled by night,
Had left the port, by morning's light
Was spied, chased, boarded—brief the fight,
But fierce as it was brief.
The crew, like tigers more than men,
Fought, though in numbers one to ten.

He who appeared their chief,
Hurled, when he saw resistance vain,
His battle-axe into the main,
And to its shattered haft was found
This missive to King Philip, bound."—(10)
"A last prayer for relief,
Or else the leaguered town must be
Straightway surrendered. Where is he
Who had this charge?" A sign; they bring
The wounded man before the King.

XIV.

"Whence and what art thou, fellow, say?"
"Thy foe!" "A harmless one to-day—
Fear'st thou not death?" "Demand of those
Who saw me at the battle's close
Wounded, weaponless, alone,
My gauntlet dash in the Gascon's face
Who dared to bid me sue for grace!"
"A sturdy knave! I like thy tone,
And pardon thy bearing frank and bold.
Edward of England thy sovereign own,
And I'll fill that gauntlet of thine with gold!"
"King! were it filled an hundredfold,

The gibbet beside, and the free choice mine,
I'd hang, ere meddle with gold of thine!"

XV.

He shook the dank locks from his brow,
As bitterly he uttered: " *Thou*
My sovereign? Read that letter—read!
If heart thou hast, that heart should bleed
At such a tale of woe.
Of pangs endured for honour's sake,
Of faith that anguish cannot shake,
However sharp the throe!
The knight hath slain his courser brave,
The page his goshawk gay,
And, wild with hunger, grudge the grave
Its feast of human clay.
Gaunt Famine stalks with ghastly stare,
And shrieks from door to door
In tones which bid the soul despair
That never quailed before.
While ye sit idly—basely—here,
And leave the Fiend to do
That work which should, with sword and spear,
Be done in fight by you!

What! Do ye fear to scale the wall
Which shadows more than men defend?
Brave spirits that upon you call,
To grant them but a warrior's end!
Ye English soldiers, up, for shame!
Mount, knights, if knights ye be!
Shout forth your boasted champion's name—
We'll answer with our old acclaim—
'Montjoye!—St. Denis!'"

XVI.

Deep silence. In an instant broken
By one loud burst of "Bravely spoken!"
"To the assault!" But Edward raised
His hand, the while he gravely gazed
Upon the captive, who, o'er-wrought
With his great effort, staggering sought
The nearest archer's arm to stay
Himself from falling. "Nay, sirs, nay!
You have our will already heard;
The town is ours without a blow,
And heaven forbid, for idle word,
One drop of English blood should flow.
As to this man"—But here the Queen,

Who mute, but not unmoved, had been
Till now spectatress of the scene,
Her hand on Edward's laid,
And whispered: " Sir, in that wan face,
The lineaments, methinks, I trace
Of one of no ignoble race."
Then, ere response was made,
Nearer the prisoner she drew,
Who gathered up his strength anew
To pay such beauty homage due,
And gently to him said :
" Art thou a knight ? "—" No, royal dame,
Such rank it is not mine to claim ;
Humble of birth as of degree,
Of Calais but a burgess free ;
A merchant, in simple sooth am I,
But not of my sword or my loyalty."

XVII.

The royal pair exchanged a glance,
Then Edward spake. " Worthy of France,
Whate'er thou art, thy speech hath won
Our favour—see his bonds undone,
Some skilful surgeon bring

To tend his wound—let him have food—
And wine, so be't the leech think good;
And with all speed, his strength renewed,
Safe conduct to his king.
Burgess, farewell! To Philip hie,
Bid him to this sad prayer reply;
And say that England knows
How to respect true bravery,
E'en in her fiercest foes."
Again the silver trumpets sound,
Again to horse the nobles bound,
Again is heard the marshal's cry,
As sweeps the proud procession by,
And scarce hath passed, before
Divested of degrading chain,
Reckless of hunger and of pain,
Gaultier la Motte stands free again
Upon that sandy shore.

XVIII.

Gaultier la Motte. In Calais town
For kindness, courage, truth, well known
Was he who bore that name.
For all that gives to manhood worth,

Nobility, to which no birth,
Although the highest upon earth,
Alone can found a claim.
Upon *his* birth there was a blot,
But who in Calais knew it not,
Or valued less for it La Motte?
For in those days of yore,
Of lawless love the luckless shoot
Was not dishonoured by its root,
But prized according to the fruit
Or flower that it bore.
And many the bright eyes that cast
A brighter glance as Gaultier passed,
And many a rosy cheek would burn
With deeper red, did Gaultier turn
To greet its owner fair.
All, save the only eyes whose light
He worshipped—save the cheek at sight
Of which his own would feel the blood
Mount to it like a boiling flood,
Then rush back to his labouring heart,
And leave him pale as though the dart
Of Death had smote him there!

XIX.

And yet, no bootless wooer he;
His true love's course *had* smoothly run;
His bride betrothed, full soon to be
His own for ever, he had won
Her bravely. In the fatal strife
At Cressy, he had saved the life
Of her dear father. In return,
Good old Sir Bardo de Bellebourne (")
Gave, what he loved still more than life,
His only child to be the wife
Of Gaultier de La Motte, who long
Had sighed in silence 'mid the throng
Of gay gallants who strove in vain
The hand of Lady Blanche to gain;
Nor when that hand was given away
By her fond sire, did she betray
Aught like repugnance or dismay.
Calmly—nay, as if nothing loth,
With maidenly obedience meek,
To Gaultier plighted she her troth.
But from that hour, 'twas marked, her cheek
By nature pale, still paler grew,

And the dark fringes of her eyes
Closed to retain the pearly prize.
A tear would sometimes struggle through,
Quickly, ere farther it could stray,
Brushed with a sweet, faint smile away.
But true love's eyes are in the heart,
And though so blind at times they be,
Too keen the glances they can dart,
Too plain the cruel sights they see.
And when that passive hand he took,
And gazed into that face so fair,
The heart of Gaultier at one look
Read hers, and sickened with despair!

XX.

He saw reliance on his truth,
Pride in her suitor's well-earned fame,
Esteem for one who from his youth
Had never known a breath of blame;
And for the friend who bled to shield
Her wounded sire, and for him hewed
A passage from that gory field,
A daughter's deepest gratitude.

But what were these to him—oh, what?
Who looked for Love, and found it not!

XXI.

Loved she another? No. He spurned
The hideous thought! Blanche give her hand
To him the while her young heart burned
With love for living man beside,
Even though it were un-returned?
Ah, no! He knew her well. Too grand
Her nature—she had sooner died!
But what, if him she loved were dead,
And her heart buried in his grave,
By gratitude and duty led,
All she had left to give, she gave?

XXII.

It might be so,—and shudderingly
He searched *his* heart for the reply
To the dread question, what should be
His course, while still his course was free?
Resign the hand, so lately prest
With transport to his throbbing breast?
Release her from her pledge, and fly

Where he might hide his misery
From her and all whom it might pain ?
Or blindness to her secret feign,
And wed as 'twere a marble wife,
Without Pygmalion's power to warm
The heartless statue into life
And love which gives to life its charm ?

XXIII.

Might she not love him yet ? That hope
He grasped at as the drowning man
Clutches the timely wafted rope,
Which, if it part not, save him can !
Yes ! Such should his devotion be,
His tender, unobtrusive care,
That drop by drop insensibly
His love the stone away should wear,
And fall like balm upon the wound
Which only love like his had found.
But this was not a time to wed,
When foreign foes, with swords still red
With blood at fatal Cressy shed,
Around the city prest.
And Gaultier felt almost relief

That Blanche had gained a respite brief,
Nor let one sigh of selfish grief
Escape his generous breast.

XXIV.

Weeks, months wore on, and day by day
The hope of succour fainter grew,
And vainly in the distance grey
King Philip's friendly banners flew.
Closely begirt by land and sea,
Unable or to fight or flee,
Silent and stern, still unsubdued,
The scanty band of heroes stood,
Enduring to the last.
While crowds were clamouring for bread,
And mothers with their babes unfed,
With wolfish eyes glared on the dead
As they were hurried past,
And pestilence began to tread
In famine's footsteps fast.

XXV.

Then issued was the stern decree,
By merciless necessity

From lips unwilling wrung.
Of either sex, the sick, the poor,
All who of food had not some store,
The aged and the young—
Full seventeen hundred souls were driven,
Without an hour of warning given,
Forth from the city gate,
To meet at England's hands, whate'er
Might urge, in hasty council there,
Her mercy or her hate.
Oh! be it told to England's fame,
What of that houseless host became.
Welcomed and feasted, tended, cheered,
As they had nearest kindred been,
Brothers they found in foes they feared,
Bounty where they but bonds had seen,
Alms for their momentary need,
Safe conduct, and a kind " God speed! " (¹²)

XXVI.

Meanwhile in Calais rose a cry
Of anguish and dismay.
" Blanche de Bellebourne ! " and no reply
That could a father's agony,

A lover's dread allay!
In vain they seek—in vain they call—
She is not in the old dark hall,
Nor in the dainty chamber small,
Where she was fain to bide,
'Mid bright hued birds and fragrant flowers,
And all that makes of Beauty's bowers
The pleasure and the pride.
The portal none have seen her pass—
Went she to mart?—Went she to mass?
No tidings can they gain.
And through the city far and wide,
Without the faintest clue to guide,
By day, by night, the quest is plied,
Nor left unsearched or unespied
A nook in which a gnat could hide,
But all in vain!—In vain!

XXVII.

Gone! Fled! Not fled! It could not be!
What earthly cause for flight had she?
Each asked, nor answer found.
Though Gaultier's brain began to burn
With doubt his love still strove to spurn,

But which would ruthlessly return
His loyal heart to wound.
When lo! a sudden gleam of light
Flashed through the hourly deepening night
Of his despair. That morn she might,
On kindly errand bound,
To succour some poor soul in need,
The sick to cheer, the hungry feed—
As was her daily wont indeed—
Have left her father's house unseen,
And in a luckless moment been
Entangled in the wretched crowd
That onwards, amid wailings loud,
Were hurried to the gate,
And through it in confusion thrust,
Amid the human torrent, must
Have shared the common fate!

XXVIII.

Then there was hope, for well was known
The kindness to those outcasts shown,
And Blanche de Bellebourne—Hah!—but here
The hope was shadowed by a fear!
Too fair a captive to set free,

The kindness shown to her might be
Closely allied to cruelty.
Were she for ransom but detained,
Some tidings had ere now been gained.
Still there was hope; a bark he knew,
Manned by a sturdy-hearted few,
Awaited but the chance to steal
Out of the port some misty night,
And running past Wissant, ere light
Should to the fleet betray their flight,
Send one to bear, as best he might,
A letter with a last appeal
From valiant old Jean de Vienne ([13])
Unto his Sovereign Liege,
Who with full sixty thousand men
Inactive lay within the ken
Of sore-prest Calais, which had then
Endured a twelvemonth's siege.
That letter Gaultier prayed to bear.
Right glad were they to grant his prayer,
For who more brave than he?
With one accord their captain made,
As sank the moon they anchor weighed,
And out they stood to sea.

XXIX.

What fate that daring bark befell,
Reader, thou know'st already well.
Return we therefore to the strand,
Where Gaultier by the king's command
Was from his fetters freed.
A careful leech had dressed and bound
His deep, but not disabling wound.
Reposed, refreshed, for him is found
An easy ambling steed,
Whereon, as in the rosy sky
The first pale star of evening shines,
His friendly foes escorted by,
He passes through the English lines;
But not before frank answer given
To every question he could frame,
Well-nigh away the doubts had driven
That on his spirit crowding came.
Of Blanche, not one had heard the name.
No whisper of a captive fair,
No rumour of a high-born maid
Amid the squalid wretches there,
So lately granted food and aid.

If such an one o'erlooked had been,
She must have quitted with the rest,
And gaining Philip's camp unseen,
Perchance was now his honoured guest.

XXX.

Lighter of heart, he bids adieu
Those rough but honest yeomen to,
And the last English barrier through,
He gives his steed the rein.
And soon he hears the sullen flow (¹⁴)
Of the vexed river struggling slow,
Through swamp and beach, itself to throw
Into the moaning main.
And on the ridge beyond, a row
Of tents like sheeted spectres show,
Or distant mountain peaks of snow,
Beneath the rising moon.
And watch fires fling their ruddy glow
Upon the barren waste below,
Salt marsh and sandy dune.

XXXI.

The sudden glitter of a lance,
Stern challenge and brief answer : " France ! "
But still, ere suffered to advance,
Close question'd, strictly scanned.
Onward commanded then to ride,
A mounted spearman by his side,
Who seemed his captor more than guide,
So jealously his charge he eyed.
Along the dreary road they pass,
By stunted bush and scanty grass,
Alone marked out through deep morass,
Till at the foot they stand
Of one of those low hills that lie
Darkly against the pale blue sky,
Where day hath scarce had time to die,
And o'er their heads behold
The camp of Philip de Valois,
And the proud " Pavillon du Roi,"
Which all of purple cloth of gold,
Powdered with fleurs-de-lys untold,
Softly besilvered by the moon,
Shone like a winter sun at noon

The humbler tents above.
The wished-for goal is seen at last,
Almost within a javelin's cast,
And Gaultier mounts the easy slope,
Guided by Honour, cheered by Hope,
And nerved with even Fate to cope,
By Fate's sole master—Love !

XXXII.

Ay, master ! For love true and pure
As Gaultier's, though it may not cure
The wounds of Fate, it can *endure*.
And in that unrelenting war,
To bear is to be conqueror.
Time cannot wear it from the heart;
Distance divides, but cannot part,
Absence no change can in it make,
Falsehood e'en fails its faith to shake,
Peril but renders it more brave,
Love strong as death defies the grave ;
The earth may shrivel like a scroll—
Love is immortal as the soul !

NOTES TO CANTO 1.

Page 9, line 1.

(¹) "*It is a lovely summer day.*"

In order to concentrate the action of the story, I have taken the liberty to bring Queen Philippa to Calais a few days only previous to the surrender of the town, instead of shortly after the commencement of the siege. No important historical fact is affected by the supposition.

Page 9, line 10.

(²) "*Cape Blanez.*"

The Capes Blanez (Blanc-nez) and Grisnez are two well-known headlands west of Calais, and the nearest points to the English coast.

Page 10, line 6.

(³) "*Wissant's harbour deep,
And Sangatte's castle-crowned steep,
And Nieulay's moated wall.*"

To modern travellers, who may perchance have visited these places, it may be necessary to state that Wissant was in the fourteenth century a port as much frequented as our own of Sandwich on the opposite coast, now equally choked up by the accumulation of sand. It was at Wissant that Queen Philippa landed, and took up her abode at the Castle of Sangatte, which at that period dominated the little fishing village of that name; but razed to the ground by the Duke de Guise in 1558, no trace of its site remains. The fort of Nieulay still exists, but its architectural features have no similarity to those it presented in 1347.

Page 11, line 18.

(⁴) "*King Edward's wooden town.*"

"On the king's arrival before Calais he laid siege to it, and built between it and the river and bridge houses of wood. They were laid out in streets and thatched with straw or broom, and in this town of the King's there was everything necessary for an army, besides a market-place, where there were markets every Wednesday and Saturday for butchers' meat and all other sorts of merchandise. Cloth, bread, and everything else that came from England and Flanders might be had there as well as all comforts for money."—*Froissart,* book i. cap. 132.

Page 12, line 8.

(⁵) "*Who made the Scottish Lion quail before the Leopards three.*"

The battle of Neville's Cross, near Durham, in which the Scotch were defeated, and their king, David, was taken prisoner by the English forces, raised, if not actually commanded in person, by Queen Philippa, was fought on Saturday, October 17, 1346.

Page 14, line 2.

(⁶) ——— "*the Black Prince for ever!*"

The origin of this popular epithet has never been satisfactorily accounted for, and the earliest mention of it yet discovered is in a document of the reign of his son Richard II.; but from the manner in which it is there introduced it is clear that it must have been at that period an appellation perfectly familiar to the public, and therefore probably conferred on him during his lifetime. Some writers have imagined that it was given to him by the French in consequence of the calamities his valour had entailed upon them. Others, that it arose from the colour of the habiliments he usually wore, the field of his " arms of peace," as he calls them in his will, being *sable*, and I have consequently described his dress according to that idea. In no representation of him, however, either in armour or civil attire, and there are many of them besides his effigy in Canterbury Cathedral, is there anything to be found to corroborate the suggestion.

Page 14, line 17.

(7) "*Had foul dishonour wept* ———"

The chivalric protection of the two handsome daughters of the Count de Poix by the Lord Basset and Sir John Chandos, from the violence of the soldiers during the march of the English army through Picardy, after the battle of Caen, is recorded by Froissart in the 124th chapter of his 1st book.

Page 15, line 22.

(8) ——— "*points to statutes vain.*"

The poets and chroniclers of the fourteenth century are loud in their lamentations over the extravagant fashions of the day, amongst which the peculiar one of cutting the edges of sleeves and other portions of their garments into the shape of leaves and various other fantastic devices, is specially prohibited to certain classes in the sumptuary laws of that period, which ineffectually endeavoured to restrain " the sinful costly array of clothing."

Page 17, line 19.

(9) ——— "*on Sangatte's hill*
Philip of France is lingering still."

The King of France and his army passed through the country of Fawkenberg and came straight to the hill of Sangatte, between

Calais and Wissant. . . . When those in Calais perceived them from the walls pitching their tents, they thought it had been a new siege."—*Froissart*, book i. chap. 143.

Page 20, line 5.

(¹⁰) "*Hurled, when he saw resistance vain,
His battle-axe into the main,
And to its shattered haft was found
This missive to King Philip, bound.*"

This anecdote is related by the old chronicler Avesbury, fol. 157 King Edward forwarded the letter.

Page 26, line 8.

(¹¹) "*Brave old Sir Bardo de Bellebourne.*"

The real name of this personage appears, by Buchon's admirable edition of Froissart, to have been "Badouin de Bellebrunne." I have, however, availed myself of Mr. Johnes's inaccuracy in order to avoid palming a fictitious story on an historical family.

Page 31, line 18.

(¹²) "*Safe conduct, and a kind 'God speed!*'"

"When the Governor of Calais saw the preparations of the King of England, he collected together all the poor inhabitants who had not laid in any store of provisions, and one Wednesday morning sent upwards of seventeen hundred men, women, and children, out of the town. As they were passing through the English army they were asked why they had left the town ; they replied because they had nothing to eat. The king upon this allowed them to pass through in safety, ordered them a substantial dinner, and gave to each two sterlings as charity and alms, for which many of them prayed earnestly for the king."—*Froissart*, book i. chap. 138.

THE BURGESS.

Page 34, line 13.

(¹³) "*Valiant old Jean de Vienne.*"

"A Burgundy knight, named Sir John de Viènne, was Governor of Calais, and with him were Sir Arnold D'Andreghem, Sir John de Surie, Sir Bardo de Bellebourne, Sir Geoffrey de la Motte, Sir Pepin de Were, and many other knights and squires."—*Froissart*, chap. 132.

Page 36, line 9.

(¹⁴) "*And soon he heard the sullen flow
Of the vexed river*" ———

The little river of Hames, between which and the river of Guines the English forces were encamped. There was a bridge over it at Fort Nieulay, which was strongly guarded by the Earl of Derby being the only practicable road from Sangatte to Calais.

CANTO THE SECOND.

THE MINSTREL.

CANTO THE SECOND.

THE MINSTREL.

I.

Upon a cliff below Blanez
A minstrel sat at close of day,
Amid a mingled throng
Of armed men from camp and fort,
Sailors and fishers from the port,
Chapmen from the Ville de Bois,
Pedlars from Flanders and Artois,
Pages, varlets, peasant churls,
Wrinkled crones, and blooming girls,
Mute, listening to his song.

II.

Youthful, but manly was his mien;
Tall, fair, blue-eyed, he had, I ween,
Scarce two-and-twenty summers seen.
Clothed in a coat-hardie of green,

With hood and hosen grey.
From silken cord upon his breast,
Hung, of his harp the silver wrest
By minstrel worn alway. (¹)
'Twas said he had been born in France,
And in that cradle of romance,
That sunny land of song, Provence,
From boyhood wooed the " gai science,"
And featly could he play
On harp and regal, gittern, lute,
Nor sing alone; but make, to boot,
Sirvente and Virelai.
To England on some mission bound,
With England's Queen he favour found,
And in that royal lady's train
Now treads his native land again.

III.

" Of battle and of chivalry,
Of ladie's love and drucrie,"
As old Dan Chaucer writes, could he
In tuneful numbers tell,
But love was aye his favourite theme,
And then his large blue eyes would beam

With light his hearers well might deem
From Love's high-altar fell.
And when he sang his lady's praise
Those eyes to Heaven he seemed to raise,
As if they only there could see
A being fair and pure as she.
But, oh! so tender of her fame,
He never breathed that lady's name;
By lips profane to hear it spoken,
Methinks his gentle heart had broken.

IV.

And what his own? Guillaume was all
The name that he had e'er let fall;
But English tongues soon 'gan him call
" Young William with the Ring."
For on his finger day and night
He wore an emerald which might
Have graced that of a king!
The hoop this posy round it bore,—
"EN . LOYAL . AMOUR . TOUT . MON . CŒUR,"
And when he thought that none were nigh,
To scan his acts with curious eye,
That gem he to his lips would press

With reverential tenderness,
And seemingly with prayers address,
As 'twere a living thing.
And the gay witlings of the Court,
Who fain had of the youth made sport,
Felt the jest die upon their tongue
If but a glance on them he flung;
For something in those earnest eyes
Made them less mirthful, if not more wise.

V.

It surely needs not me to tell
How gentle dame and demoiselle
Looked on that minstrel boy;
For he in sooth was scarcely more
When first he sought on English shore
Protection or employ.
So young, so ardent, yet so grave;
Meek as a maid, yet brave.—Oh! brave—
You could not doubt—as the best knight
That ever shivered lance in fight!
Worshipping one, as 'twas his pride
In song to blazon far and wide,
But ice itself to all beside.

Yet kind and courteous to each and all,
Sat they in bower or served they in hall.
And let but woman high or low,
Or suffer wrong or meet with woe,
None prompt as William with the Ring,
Forward with heart and arm to spring
To aid, console, defend.
Add to all this the witching tone
Of that sweet voice which seemed Love's own,
The mystery around him thrown,—
A veil which none could rend—
And lives there woman young or old,
I ask again, who need be told
How many hearts for Guillaume glowed,
How many tears for Guillaume flowed,
When homeward called to wend?

VI.

Three years have come and gone since he
Sat on the cliff beside the sea
Where now he sits again,
Enchanting with his minstrelsy
The motley groups that stand or lie
Around him on that headland high,

Far beetling o'er the main.
It is a spot a bard would choose
On which to woo his darling muse;
On such a day—at such an hour.
The crimson sun is sinking low,
The western sky is all a-glow,
And the sea slumbers far below
In the full consciousness of power.
The tide is out—you cannot hear
The hush of the retreating waves,
Scarce see their tiny crests uprear,
As each at leaving, fondly laves
Once more the smooth and glittering sand
That circles like a silver band
The lonely, lovely bay.
Beyond it, one unbroken green,
The ocean stretches, still, serene,
On either hand away,
And rising from it like a ghost,
The white line of the English coast
Appears in that delusive light
So near, you'd deem an urchin might
Without an effort, from his bow,
A bird-bolt o'er it fairly throw.

VII.

But the rapt minstrel sees it not,
Earth, sky and ocean, all forgot;
In a far dream-land of his own.
He wanders amid scenes unknown
To duller sons of clay,
While mute and motionless around,
As if by spell of wizard bound,
The crowd expectant stay.
Suddenly, starting from his trance,
With kindling cheek and flashing glance,
The harp that had beside him lain
He presses to his heart again ;
Again he sweeps the sounding string,
Again of love he yearns to sing.
Ye whose young hearts are on the wing,
Listen to William with the Ring,
And profit by his lay.

VIII.

THE MINSTREL'S SONG.

Love ! 'Tis a word that's lightly said,
But a heavy heart by it oft is made.
Weigh it, ere from thy lips it fall—
It may but be liking after all !
Liking, because of a laughing eye—
Liking because none fairer be nigh,
Liking that ends with the next day's light,
But leaves a mourner in endless night !

Love ! There is music in the word !
From the rudest lip with a thrill 'tis heard ;
Ponder, ere in thy heart it sink,
It may not be love as thou fain would'st think.
True to the ear is the tender tone,
But if it spring from the lips alone,
With a breath it came,—with a breath 'twill fly—
And leave thee to weep o'er that word for aye !

IX.

Solemn as sweet the warning fell
On some who heard him like a knell,

And o'er their cheeks though passed a smile,
Tears glistened in their eyes the while.
Even the rough and reckless there,
Who last would for the counsel care,
Owned of that voice the magic rare—
The Bard's consummate art—
And all with praise, and some with pence,
Would of his merit mark their sense.
The coin he courteously declined,
The praise received with grace refined,
Then rose as to depart.
And homeward down the steep descent
The scattering crowd their footsteps bent
To harbour, camp, or mart.
In silence first—they knew not why,
But laugh, and shout, and ribaldry,
And banter coarse, and jest profane
Soon turned the tide of thought again,
And from the memory swept away
Alike the lesson and the lay,

X.

The bard was left alone. His hood
Thrown back, with upturned eyes he stood,

And folded hands, as if in prayer.
The sun, upon his golden hair
A parting stream of glory shed.
There seemed a halo round his head!
More saint-like form in holy fane
Ne'er shone in painted window-pane,
And yet, to speak the simple sooth,
Not Heavenward did his spirit soar.
On earth amid the scenes of youth
He sought one image evermore,
And Love, and Purity, and Truth
Gave him the look divine he wore!

XI.

His soul had fled from that bleak rock
To leafy bowers far away,
A lovely vale in Languedoc,
Where once again he seemed to stray
With a fair, fragile, gentle girl,
Whose cheeks as pale as purest pearl
Gave somewhat more of light and size
To her large, lustrous, hazel eyes.
The raven tresses, which unbound,
Would in rich masses touch the ground,

The swan-like neck, the fairy feet,
The tiny hand so quick to meet
His own, and locked within it lie
While hours unnumbered flitted by.
All this again was present—near—
Her very voice he seemed to hear.

XII.

From infancy together reared,
A foundling on the bounty thrown
Of her brave sire whom he revered—
Her mother loved too, as his own—
That little maiden, sweet and mild,
Had been his idol from a child,
And she had from her tenderest age
Clung fondly to her pretty page,
For such her father made the boy,
To the poor orphan's pride and joy.
Thus early in their bosoms both,
That first love sown, grew with their growth
And strengthen'd with their strength;
They never sought that love to mask,
No questions dreaded they to ask
Till the time came at length—

As it was sure to come—when each
Became more guarded in their speech,
And she would turn away her eyes
When his too clearly in them saw,
And the small hand he made his prize
Almost reproachingly withdraw.
Upon their love had dawned a light
Which made them tremble at its sight!

XIII.

Her mother was a saint in Heaven,
Who would have pitied and forgiven;
Fond as he was of her, her sire,
Proud, passionate, and rash as fire,
As fierce and reckless in his rage
As when unruffled, kind and sage,
Although he really loved the youth,
Would ne'er receive him as his son,
And should he but suspect the truth,
His fury —— What was to be done?
Part!—At once. Hard as it might seem,
It left of hope some little gleam.
Guillaume his parents never knew,
But to that knowledge had a clue

Lightly regarded hitherto,
Of mighty import now.
In England, friends he yet might trace
To prove he was of noble race,
Then boldly to her father's face
He might his love avow,
No more a foundling page who owed
Service for charity bestowed,
But one whose rank and wealth perchance
Might claim the fairest hand in France!

XIV.

They parted—if it be to part
Still to live in each other's heart,
For ever one dear face behold,
For ever one dear form enfold,
One voice for ever seem to hear,
As on that barren mountain brow,
Her silver accents in the ear
Of the young bard seemed thrilling now.
Seemed ?—Holy Mary!—Was it seeming ?
Never was yet such truthful dreaming!
For at that instant rose a strain,
As if from out the sleeping main,

The well-remembered rondelai,
The song which he so oft had heard
Her sing, in that long byegone day—
Aye!—Note for note and word for word!

XV.

RONDELAI. (²)

Return, my love! Thou stay'st
Too long from me,
Sorrow the heart doth waste
That yearns for thee;
My spirit on thee calleth night and day,
Return, my love! Thou stay'st too long away!

Nought to my bosom brings
A comfort true,
When wanting thee, all things
Seem wanting too!
Save hope, and that is dying, day by day!
Return, my love! Thou stay'st too long away!

XVI.

Statue like—rooted to the ground,
While floated yet that voice around,

Sweet as a silver bell;
Breathless, as though he feared a word,
The slightest sound the air that stirred,
Would break the wondrous spell,
The Minstrel stood. An awe profound
Upon his senses fell.
Alone, upon that lofty height,
No human form within his sight,
No tree, no bush, no stone that might
A human form conceal:
One only thought his mind possessed—
Dead!—From its earthly shackles freed,
Out of the mansions of the blessed,
It was her spirit called indeed,
And chiding his delay
To join her in those bright domains,
Where perfect love for ever reigns,
Thus summon'd him away.

XVII.

It ceased, and starting from his trance,
He cast a wild and wistful glance
Up to the solemn sky,
Wherein one star, alone as yet,

Was like a brilliant beryl set,
Then with a piercing cry
Of " Blanche !—I come ! " he forward sprang
To the cliff's crumbling brink,
When, as in answer to it, rang
A shriek which made him shrink
Back from the dreadful dizzy height,
While from its chalky verge to sight
Arose a face almost as white.
" Guillaume ! "— In vain reply
His lips would frame—they fail to meet—
His o'erfraught heart forgets to beat,
And he falls senseless at her feet.

XVIII.

Slowly his eyes unclose to find
Her arms around his neck entwined,
His brow with tears are wet.
Delicious tears, their birth that owe
To the heart's sudden overflow
By joy, unlooked for, met.
'Tis Blanche herself beside him kneels,
His living, loving Blanche is there;
The beating of her heart he feels,

About him falls her fragrant hair,
No mocking phantom this.
Her breath is warm upon his cheek,
His own comes thick—he cannot speak—
But with a thrill of bliss
So exquisite 'tis almost pain,
He folds her to his heart again.

XIX.

When words at length he found: "Oh read
This riddle, dearest Blanche!" he cried;
"How cam'st thou here? and whence the need
Of this strange guise?" For him beside
A stripling seemed to stand.
A youth arrayed in such attire
As boatmen wore upon that coast,
Who plied their humble craft for hire
Between the fleet and land.
Some fisherman, belike, his sire,
Or Calais pilot at the most,
So like a ship-boy clad was she
In gown of falding to the knee, (³)
Where by wide supple boots 'twas met.
A leathern belt by bosses set,

A cord across her shoulder flung,
In which a naked dagger swung.
A woollen cap of dusky red
Poised jauntily upon her head.
But that the glossy raven hair,
Which had escaped its bandage, streamed
Down to her feet, as though it were
A silken mantle, none had dreamed
That she was aught but what her dress
Proclaimed her in its simpleness.

XX.

Her finger on her lip she placed,
And to the cliff's extremest edge
Her footsteps cautiously retraced,
And pointed to a shelving ledge
Which jutted out from its sheer side,
It might be half a spear's length wide,
Invisible save to the sight
Of those who dared approach so near
The crumbling brink of that dread height
Its very verge to over-peer.
Of stairs rough hewn in it, a flight
Led to a hut which from the sea,

A black spot 'gainst that mass of white
In air suspended seemed to be,
Beneath the crag's o'erhanging crest.
Some solitary sea bird's nest,
Or eagle's erie, rather than
A habitation made for man.

XXI.

More nearly viewed, the shapeless speck
The spoils display'd of many a wreck,
Uncouthly heaped, as though the blast
In sport the ruins up had cast
Of each unhappy barque,
Upon that narrow shelf to form
A quaint memorial of the storm,
Half hovel and half ark.
A boat keel upwards for a roof,
The ribs of some old coasting craft
For walls, scarce rendered weather proof
By portions of a rotten raft
Against them nailed, strained over which
Was sail-cloth coated well with pitch.
The grating from a hatchway reft
For window served and chimney too.

So clogged with soot, scant room was left
For light or smoke to struggle through.
The door, a cabin door had been
Of a gay Spanish galleon,
Or one of those proud argosies,
Venetian or Genoese,
With costly wares for England bound,
Which on that coast its fate had found;
For some faint traces still, thereon,
Of paint and gilding might be seen.
And as on rusty hinge it swung
It seemed to mourn its altered fate,
And groan in some outlandish tongue
Of perished wealth and altered state.

XXII.

Adown the treacherous descent,
Light as a fay the maiden went,
Followed, as if in some strange dream,
By Guillaume, who still scarcely knew,
'Mid all these marvels, what to deem
Delusion, what to trust as true.
And feared to see that form so fair
Melt the next moment into air.

They reached the hut and entered. There
On the bare earth, for floor was none,
Smouldered a fire, a fitful glare
Flinging a motley mass upon
Of nets and cordage, boat-hooks, oars,
Casks, hampers, filled with damaged stores,
Hung on the blackened walls or piled
Against them in confusion wild.
But clear enow the tale they told,
Of struggles fierce with Ocean, wroth
To lose its prey by mortals bold,
Fishers or wreckers—one or both.

XXXIII.

The maiden seized a smoky torch
That burned beside the low-browed porch,
And raised with effort slight
The lid of a large oaken chest,
Which, as a spring within she prest,
Self-acting glided from its place,
Leaving to view an open space
And of a spiral stair the head,
Down which by the red light
Of the rude torch again she led

The minstrel with amazement dumb.
Down, down, and down, it seemed as though
To the earth's centre they would go,
And near it must have come,
But that at intervals the air
Swept in light gusts through loopholes small,
And caused the murky torch to flare,
And dance their shadows on the wall.
And now and then his eye,
Caught through the aperture a star
That tremulously glittered far—
Far off in the blue sky;
While more distinctly on his ear
The murmur of the ocean fell,
Mysteriously, as you may hear
What seems its echo in a shell.

XXIV.

The lowest step is gained at length,
Facing a door of wondrous strength,
With iron clamped and nails as thick
As in a target set.
The heaviest axe—the strongest pick
Its master there had met.

Lightly upon it thrice the maid
Smote with the hilt of her dagger small;
Quickly the signal was obeyed—
Bolts were withdrawn—chains heard to fall,
A key creaked in the lock.
The ponderous portal backward thrown,
A vaulted cave was dimly shown,
By Nature's cunning hand alone
Scooped out of the huge rock.
Through its low arched mouth you might
See, glittering 'neath the rising moon,
A narrow creek with boulders white
And rocky fragments thickly strewn.
As if some crag to pieces hewn,
Or shattered by the lightning stroke,
Had hopelessly essayed
With its own ruins up to choke
The gap its fall had made.

XXV.

Spacious the cavern—sight in vain
Its deep recesses would explore,
Light from without could entrance gain
But some few paces from the shore.

Suspended by an iron chain
Flickered a lamp a niche before,
Wherein of sculpture quaint and rude
An image of our Lady stood.
It glimmered feebly in the glare
Shed by the torch which freer air
More freely caused to burn. The flame
Shone full upon an ancient dame,
Poorly but neatly clad ; her garb
A widow's by the plaited barbe,
Who with respectful gesture took
From Blanche the torch, and, with the look
Of one who danger from it feared,
Extinguished it——Secured again
The door by lock, and bolt, and chain,
Then in the darkness disappeared.

XXVI.

Then Blanche de Bellebourne silence broke ;
Hurriedly of the past she spoke,
Told briefly how her father brought
His twenty lances to the field,
And how at Cressy he had fought,
And there had sooner died than yield,

But rescued, had in Calais found
Jean de Vienne, his ancient friend,
And with him as in honour bound
Remained, the city to defend.
How she had left the dear old tower
In Languedoc to share the fate
Of her chivalric sire.
And how one morn in luckless hour,
She had been thrust from out the gate,
And here, in male attire,
With humble friends had refuge ta'en,
Tempted—and as she spake her cheek
Flushed slightly—with them to remain
Awhile, and thus disguisèd seek
The truth to learn of a report
Which by the breath of common fame,
Wafted from shore to shore,
Of a mysterious minstrel came
In favour high at England's court,
Whose age, appearance, nation, name,
The shadow raised of hope long fled,
The spectre of one wept as dead
Three weary years and more.

XXVII.

Dead! and his letter?—She had ne'er
Received it. Trusted to the care
Of pilgrim to Loretto bound,
The bearer death himself had found,
A dreadful death, upon the way,
Burned in the hostel where he lay.
But why from silence glean
That he had perished? Not alone
From silence. 'Twas too surely known
The bark in which he sailed had been
Upon the fatal Goodwins thrown
In the tempestuous night,
And e'er morn broke upon the wave
Had sunk into that sandy grave,
With every soul from sight!

XXVIII.

"Not so, sweet Blanche! My love for thee
Sustained me in the surging sea,
Amid the horrors of the storm
All radiant shone that angel form!
Amid the blackness of the night .

Those eyes to me were beacons bright,
That hope, and strength, and courage gave
To battle with the whelming wave,
And when the day brought timely aid,
To Heaven my grateful thanks were paid—
Not that for my poor life it cared,
But for the pangs thy heart was spared!"

XXIX.

" And see," he cried, " how that same love
Has triumphed fortune's spite above,
And given me that will blessed make
The life it saved for thy sweet sake!"
A parchment from his breast he took,
He marked not her despairing look,
Nor how her frame with terror shook;
All glowing with delight and pride
The precious scroll alone he eyed.
" Yes, dearest Blanche, the proof is here.
No more thy father's frown I fear,
Broad lands are mine, with tower and town,
A coronet thy brows shall crown;
Amid the first in rank and fame
The heralds will thy style proclaim,

' Place for the high and noble dame,
Blanche, wife of Guillaume de Brienne,
Viscount of Guines and Meaux,
Lord of Hames, Andres, Balinghen,
Bonningues and Bouquehaut!' (⁴)
Not that the crown of France, one grace
Could add to that enchanting face;
Nor all the kingdom's wealth impart
More value to that constant heart!"

XXX.

"My own!—For ever now my own!"
And in his arms he clasped
Her shrinking form. A piteous moan,
From lips as white and cold as stone,
Startled him, as she strove to break
From his embrace. "For mercy's sake
What ails thee, Blanche?" Feebly she spake—
"Oh there are pangs which, worse than death"—
She paused abruptly, and for breath
A moment wildly gasped;
Her eyes were dry, a burning chain
Seemed tightened round her whirling brain;
With both her hands she grasped

Her head, and swayed it to and fro,
In a dumb agony of woe.

XXXI.

He bore her to a rocky seat
And knelt in terror at her feet.
" Speak to me, Blanche! What may this mean?
Fool that I am! this joy hath been
Too sudden, and her heart o'er fraught
Against the flood has vainly fought.
O, speak to me! my love! my wife!"
Through all her frame a shudder past,
A struggle, as for very life,
She made.—" It must be told at last,"
She murmured, "let what will betide."
Her arms fell listless by her side,
Her head she with an effort raised,
And miserably on him gazed
With her hot, tearless eyes. Amazed!
Alarmed! " What must be told?" he cried.
" Guillaume, I am a promised bride."
Slowly, distinctly, every word
She spoke, and he distinctly heard;
But though they seemed his blood to freeze,

Their meaning he could scarcely seize.
" True! mine! " he faltered forth at length.
" Thine! oh, Guillaume! God give us strength
This cross to bear! Our love unknown,
My sire engaged my faith, and bound
Himself by a most solemn vow."
Terribly plain their meaning now!
Up from his knees he sprang,
And with a shout that round and round
The vaulted cavern rang,
Echoed, " A vow! " Then in a tone
Of mingled anguish, wrath, and scorn,
" Thy father's vow! Where was thine own,
A thousand times so deeply sworn?
Upon this true and trusting heart
Engaged thy faith! False as thou art!
What faith is that which unredeemed
Can thus be pledged anew,—
A worthless thing that glittering seemed
A precious gem to view! "

XXXII.

He smote his brow, to which the blood
In angry haste had rushed,

And while of tears a passionate flood
From their hot fountains gushed,
" Would with the rest that I had died,
Thy falsehood all unknown !
O cruel fortune that denied
To me such lot alone !
Why save me from the sea-swept deck,
In storm like this my heart to wreck ? "
" Hear me, Guillaume ! " To rise she tried,
But her strength failed. " What should I hear?"
Sternly and bitterly he cried.
" Excuses ? Can they change thy state?
Regrets ? Like these proofs, held so dear,
They come too late ! They come too late ! "
He snatched the parchment from the sand,
Where he had dropped it in dismay,
And crushed it fiercely in his hand,
Then hurled it from him far away :
Glanced at the portal lock'd and barr'd,
The cavern's mouth then turned toward ;
But Blanche, with every nerve anew
By desperation strung,
Herself before him wildly threw,
And to his garment clung.

" Guillaume ! For pity's sake one word !
Thou wrong'st me ! Stay and hear me tell "—
" That thou'rt another's ? I have heard—
Farewell for ever, Blanche ! Farewell ! "

XXXIII.

To loose her hold as he essayed,
A hand was on his shoulder laid,
And at his throat a dagger blade
Gleamed faintly in the lamp's dull light.
At the same instant from behind,
His arms were seized and pinioned tight,
And round his wrists a cord was twined
So straitly that a giant's might
To struggle had availed him nought,
So suddenly that not a sight
Of his assailants had he caught;
And as in answer to the prayer
Of the poor maiden prostrate there,
A rough voice uttered, " Never fear,
We'll stay him for thee, Lady dear ! "
" Strike not, Marrant ! He is a friend ! "
Blanche in her terror screamed,
For o'er him, ready to descend,

Again the dagger gleamed.
"A friend? Strange friend it would appear
From what we marked. How came he here
At such a time, and to what end?
Speak, mother." For the aged dame
Back to the spot now hurrying came.
"Good son," she answered eagerly,
"He is our countryman,—well known
Both to the Lady Blanche and me."
Then drew him by the sleeve aside,
And further spake in undertone,
The while distrustfully he eyed
The minstrel, who fast bound—alone
Now left—upon his captors cast
In turn a look of helpless rage,
As forth into the light they passed
Sea-faring men of middle age,
Tall, stalwart, sunburned, wont to wage
War with the billow and the blast.
In number seven, each armèd well
With dagger, axe, and basilard—
Fellows who would in struggle hard
Their lives know stoutly how to guard,
Or dearly to the foeman sell.

As witness then the widows could
Of many an English yeoman good;
For still our annals tell
Of havoc made on sea and land
By the bold leaders of that band,
Marrant and Mestriel. (⁵)

XXXIV.

He whom the widow called her son,
Their secret conference now done,
Held with his comrades counsel brief;
Then to the maid, absorbed in grief,
Said, " Lady, if this tale be sooth,
With us must yonder springald go.
Bound as he is; 'twill test his truth,
And haply save thee deeper woe.
But let him silence keep—a breath
To cause alarm, and instant death—"
Blanche saw the angry lightning flash,
And rapidly, ere answer rash
Could follow like the thunder crash—
" Calais," she cried, " they go to save !
Already twice these seamen brave
Have into the despairing town

Unlooked-for succour timely thrown.
A third bold venture now they make,
Then not for me, but for the sake
Of gallant souls in sorest need—
Of Heaven, who hears their cries,
Imperil not by word or deed
This holy enterprise!"
He answered not, but sullenly
Let fall his head upon his breast,
Nor raised it as she timidly
Replaced the parchment in his vest.
A sudden sense of treachery
Had for an instant on him prest,
And every fibre in his frame
Now felt the tingling glow of shame.
Treason and Blanche!—ye saints above!
To couple treason with her name;
The foulest treason was to love!

XXXV.

And this was William with the Ring,
Who could of love so nobly sing.
Well might he cower beneath the eye
Of her he had wronged so grievously!

Oh human heart! Oh human heart!
A weak and wicked thing thou art.
When by the gust of passion swayed,
Of what frail stuff we find thee made!
Yet his was not the common flame
To which men give of love the name.
Well had it borne the test of time,
Of absence in a foreign clime:
Nay more, the dangerous light that lies
In melting beauty's tender eyes.
Through every trial it had past,
Unshaken save in this, the last
And fiercest. He had doubted! True,
'Twas but an instant, but he knew
His guilt, and conscience-stricken stood,
With all, but most himself at feud!

XXXVI.

Meanwhile the sailors watched the tide,
Which, rising fast, began to ride
Over the rock-strewn sand
Of that secluded cove, and make
Within its breast a tiny lake,
The waves of which would gently break

While round each bluff head land,
That started up like giants twain
To guard the entrance from the main,
The billows spent their fury vain·
In charges wild and grand.
The water mounted up and up
Till brimful seemed the craggy cup
With frosted silver; for the moon,
Which, in that miniature lagoon,
Upon her bright face loved to gaze,
Had now to struggle with her rays
Thorough a filmy veil of haze,
That, smoke-like, curling, white and thin,
Came rolling from the ocean in.
And by the time the rippling wave
Had reached the level of the cave,
So close a curtain o'er it drew
That all above was lost to view,
And flood and fog were blended so,
In one soft silvery mass below,
E'en the skilled seamen scarcely wist
Which was the water, which the mist.

XXXVII.

A cry—it might be of some bird—
Was in the distance faintly heard.
The sailors listened. Twice again
'Twas uttered, and each time more plain.
" It is the signal, friends! Full well
Thou keepest tryst, good Mestriel!"
Exclaimed Marrant, and in reply
Repeated thrice the plaintive cry.
The night-watch on the cliff would deem
It was some startled curlew's scream,
Nor pause an instant in his round
To question that familiar sound.
Not so the mariners, who knew
The mighty work they had to do.
Out of a chasm near they drew
A long and stoutly timbered boat.
" Lady, 'tis time we were afloat,
The tide is serving, and the haze
We counted on its veil provides.
Brave Mestriel for us but stays,
His vessel in the offing rides,
We once on board—by Jesu's aid "—

And here the holy sign he made—
"Another hour shall scarce be past,
Ere Calais break her fearful fast."

XXXVIII.

Thus spake the widow's son to Blanche,
The while their boat his comrades launch,
And in it at his nod, their mute
And sullen prisoner they place,
Still bound securely, hand and foot.
With scowling brow and flushing face
He crouched him down—a moment more,
And Blanche was seated by his side.
The next each man bent to his oar,
Marrant the rudder seized and cried,—
"Mother, farewell, and for us pray!
Now, yarely men!—Give way! give way!"
As though the boat alive had been,
Into the mist it seemed to spring;
One instant like a phantom seen,
Then like a phantom vanishing.
The widow turned her from the bank,
Before the Virgin's image sank
Upon her knees, and while in tears

Her aged eyes began to swim,
To that sweet intercessor's ears,
Whom most the mariner reveres,
Arose the solemn, simple hymn,—

" Ave Maria! Star of the sea!
Mother of mercy, we call upon thee!
Hear us and aid us, Virgin pure,
Notre Dame de bons seccours!"

NOTES TO CANTO II.

Page 48, line 4.

(¹) "*The silver wrest
By minstrel worn alway.*"

It is singular that though we have many figures of minstrels in the illuminations of mediæval MSS., they not only differ from each other in peculiarities of costume, but in none have I seen representations of the harp-wrest or key, which we learn from verbal descriptions was as much a general sign of their vocation as it was an indispensable assistant to their art. The person in the apparel of an ancient minstrel, who figured in the grand entertainment given by the Earl of Leicester to Queen Elizabeth, at Kenilworth Castle, had " his harp in good grace dependent before him, his wrest tyed to a green lace and hanging by." His beard " was smugly shaven," and his gown was "of Kendal green." But from a MS. of the time of Edward III. (Harleian Coll., Brit. Mus. No. 1764) we learn that in those days the minstrels wore a close fitting dress called the cotehardie. That the queen had minstrels of her own is apparent from an account rendered the 11th of that reign, in which payment of six and eightpence each is recorded to have been made to the queen's minstrels (" Ministralis Dominæ Reginæ ") for playing before the king at York. (Cotton MS., Nero cviii.)

Page 60, line 5.

(²) "*Rondelai.*"

These words are a free rendering of a song by Froissart, commencing, " Reviens ami, trop longue est ta demmeure."

Page 63, line 20.

(³) "*In gown of falding to the knee.*"

The Shipman, in Chaucer's *Canterbury Tales*, is described as wearing a gown of falding (a kind of coarse cloth) reaching to the knees, and a dagger under his arm suspended by a lace which passed round his neck.

Page 74, line 3.

(⁴) "*Viscount of Guines and Meaux,
Lord of Hames, Andres, Balinghen,
Bonningues and Bouquehaut.*"

These were all seigneuries in the Comté de Guines, and the villages are to be found in the neighbourhood of Calais to this day. Vide *Notice Historique du Calaisis*, par P. J. M. Collet, 8vo Calais, 1834.

Page 80, line 6.

(⁵) "*Marrant and Mestriel.*"

No provisions could be brought into the place but by stealth, and by means of two mariners, who were guides to such as adventured; one was named Marrant and the other Mestriel; both of them resided in Abbeville. By their means the town of Calais was frequently victualled, and by their boldness they were often in great danger, many times pursued and almost taken; but they escaped, and slew and wounded many of the English."—*Froissart*, chap. 139.

CANTO THE THIRD.

THE RIVALS.

CANTO THE THIRD.

THE RIVALS.

I.

THE bells in Calais gaily ring,
In Calais mighty bonfires fling
Their light on tower and spire,
And casks are broached, and meat and bread
To famished crowds distributed,
And grateful voices shout " Noel ! " (¹)
" Long live Marrant and Mestriel ! "
Around each flaming pyre.
Roused by the uproar and the blaze,
Their wondering foes flock forth to gaze.
" Comes Philip, then, the siege to raise ? "
They eagerly inquire.
For all have heard how Edward gave
Safe conduct to a burgess brave,
Who letters to his sovereign bore,
Immediate succour to implore,

And rapidly as fire
Throughout the camp, from man to man,
The spirit-stirring rumour ran,
That morning's sun would see advance
The many-bannered host of France,
And rival monarchs, lance to lance,
Would play war's gory game of chance
To each brave heart's desire.
Throughout the night, expectant all,
They listened for the trumpet call.
The horseman tested girth and rein,
The bill-man ground his blade again,
The archer bent his trusty yew
And looked his cloth-yard arrows to.
Ready saddled pawed the steed,
And with all pieces he might need
At hand, to arm their lord with speed,
Awaited page and squire.

II.

In Calais on that self-same night
By some was seen a touching sight,
An aged man with hair snow-white,
Unkempt and streaming wild,

Holding fast locked in his embrace
A lovely girl, down whose pale face
The big drops gave each other chase,
　As up at him she smiled.
Untasted lay beside him food
Of which in woeful need he stood;
Vainly to touch it, him they prayed,
Naught marked he but that gentle maid;
Naught but two words unceasing said,
" My child ! " " My child ! " " My child ! "

III.

The night wore on, the day drew nigh,
But few in Calais closed an eye,
Though fainter and less frequently
　The shout of joy arose.
The fires burned low ;. morn's first pale light
Streamed through the wreaths of vapour white,
That shrouded from the warder's sight
　His scarce less wakeful foes.
And now more anxiously he peers
Down through the mist; assured he hears
　The gallop of a steed.
.Nearer and nearer came the sound,

On the stone causeway clattering hard,
Now deadened upon softer ground,
Deep sand or scanty patch of sward,
But still at topmost speed.
Before his horn the warder blew,
Wide open gates and barriers flew,
Unchallenged dashed the horseman through,
For well his face the soldiers knew,
And never bridle-rein he drew,
Till at the castle door
Down from the smoking horse he sprang,
While cries of " Gaultier ! Gaultier ! " rang
From throngs that seemed to pour
From every quarter of the town,
So swiftly had the tidings flown
Of his return, though still unknown
The answer that he bore.

IV.

With head upon his daughter's breast
The poor old knight had sunk to rest,
But still in sleep his arms were fast
Around his new-found treasure cast.
Blanche heard the cries, and at the name

The pale face ashy white became!
His absence on some errand bold
Had scarce an hour to her been told,
And some there were who would maintain
That he had captured been, or slain.
Slain! How herself she hated then
That at the word her heart should leap!
The bravest and the best of men,
Who loved her with a love so deep,
Perchance was slain, and she not weep?
Yes, she did weep, but not such tears
As oft had flowed at lesser fears;
And if but captive, time was gained,
And some vague shadowy hope remained;
It had nor certain name nor shape,—
All that it whispered was—" Escape!"
One thought, at least, brought comfort sweet—
Guillaume could not his rival meet!
That solitary joy was torn
From her poor heart as soon as born,
For now, alas! Gaultier was there;
She heard his foot upon the stair—
The shouts that bade him welcome home.
Safe! free!—and where was now Guillaume?

V.

Unbound as soon as in the port
The barque beneath the ramparts lay,
Ashore he leapt, and through the fort
Without a word he strode away:
Unheeded by the busy crew,
Who work enow had still to do,
And unrestrained by Blanche, who tried
To summon up her maiden pride,
And gather from her very pain
Courage this bitter cup to drain.
Her father's joy—almost too great
To bear in his enfeebled state—
Her effort to conceal from him
The pangs with which her heart was riven—
Of some reprieve—the promise dim,
By Gaultier's absence to her given—
Had for a few brief hours combined
To calm the tumult in her mind;
But now the dread that seized her soul
Passed mortal power to control!
She started up—with what intent
She knew not. Thought in thought was lost—

Sense, in a sea of troubles tost,
Its force in fruitless efforts spent;
She looked, up-standing ghastly there,
Her fingers twisted in her hair,
The living image of despair!

VI.

The old man's sleep her rising broke,
And feebly moaning as he woke,
He fixed his eyes with fever bright
Upon La Motte the brave and good,
Who at the unexpected sight
Of Blanche, within the doorway stood
Almost as motionless and white.
" Eyes, mock me not ! " he wildly cried,
" The Lady Blanche ! " " Aye, Gaultier, aye,"
To him the aged knight replied,
All but his child's return forgot—
" Poor girl, she comes to share our lot;
To us restored, with us to die ! "
She could not speak—could scarcely stand—
When Gaultier, springing to her side,
Took tenderly her stone-cold hand,
And anxiously his darling eyed.

He marked her terror and her woe,
But their true source he could not know;
Her father's state—the fate of all
Depending on the city's fall,
A sterner heart might well appal!
No other cause he guessed.
For her still more than all afraid,
Gently and mournfully he said,
" Oh, that again to gaze on thee
Should aught like pain to Gaultier be!
Oh, that of fate I should complain
With this dear hand in mine again ! "
No marvel was her silence then,
For as that hand he pressed,
The room was filled with armèd men,
And at their head Jean de Vienne,
Who Gaultier thus addressed :—

VII.

" Welcome! welcome! Thy tidings say.
Comes Philip of France with the coming day?
Will the sun arise to the charging cry
Of Bourbon and Hainault and Burgundy?" (²)
Heavily the burgess sighed ;

Gloomily he thus replied :—
" Men of Calais, your bidding is done;
But hope for Calais there is none.
Philip of France hath your letter read;
Tears of sorrow and wrath he shed;
But unless they could wash away the foe,
Little it boots ye that to know."

VIII.

A howl of anguish, rage, and scorn
Rose from the multitude forlorn,
Through whom the cruel answer past
From lip to lip with lightning speed,
And witheringly as the blast
Of which in Libyan land we read.
The crowd that, like a surging sea,
Had poured into the castle-yard,
Now slowly and despondingly
The southern ramparts turned toward,
From which before the brightening day
The mist was melting fast away,
And from the walls a wistful glance
Cast on the distant camp of France,
Still doubting if it could be true

That crownèd king and belted knight
Could sit with sword unsheathed, to view
Such shame upon his banner light
As Christendom combined would throw,
For Calais lost without a blow.

IX.

Suddenly, from the watch-tower high
They hear the warder's joyful cry,
"France to the rescue! Philip comes!"
And hark! the distant beat of drums
Upon the morning breeze is brought!
Up, with a shout, the cry is caught
And carried to an hundred homes.
"France to the rescue! Philip comes!"
Eagerly, every eye they strain
O'er dank morass and sandy plain,
To where upon St. Martin's mount
The tents of Philip they could count.
The tents are struck! They see them fall!
They hear to horse the trumpet call!
Yes! by the shrine of Notre Dame,
Yonder waves the Oriflamme,
And flashing back the sun's first beams

Long lines of spears, like glittering streams,
Streak the hill-side with moving gold.
Pennon and banner, proud unrolled,
Fling to the breeze each broidered fold.
They march! They march! A challenge bold
In England's ears their clarions ring;
Calais to succour, comes her king!
O baffled hope!—they march indeed,
But not to succour Calais speed.
Fast in the distance dies away
The tuck of drum, the trumpet's bray;
Fast in the distance sink from sight
Banners broad and lances bright.

X.

What tongue the deep despair can tell [3]
Which then upon the bravest fell?
No piteous wail, no curses loud,
Broke from that hope-abandoned crowd!
Each looked into the other's face,
Some shadow of a doubt to trace;
And when no comfort there they found,
Bent their dull eyes upon the ground
In silence, which, for depth and gloom,

Could scarce be equalled in the tomb.
But as in tropic isle doth reign
A stillness awful and profound,
Before the sweeping hurricane
Whirls in its frantic fury round :
As not a blade of grass is stirred,
Nor tiniest leaf upon the tree,
Ceases·to twitter every bird,
Hush'd is the burden of the bee,
Until the sudden burst is heard
Of rushing wind and roaring sea ;
So did that gloomy silence form
A prelude to the pending storm.

XI.

Not long the pause. When forth it broke,
'Twas as if with one voice alone
The throng, one word in thunder spoke.
A word till then unbreathed, unknown,
" Surrender ! " But so stern the tone—
More like a menace than a moan
Sounded that cry, so hardly wrung
From gallant hearts to madness stung !
Gaultier, who foremost to the wall

Had hastened at the warder's call,
And, like the rest, with false hope flushed,
Had sickened as he felt it crushed,
Strove eagerly, but all in vain,
A hearing from the crowd to gain.
" Rather," he shouted, " let us fly
To arms! The land-gates open throw,
And in one glorious sally die,
Each on the body of a foe!"

XII.

They heard him not; or, if they heard,
Replied but with the self-same word,
" Surrender!" Shout succeeded shout,
And rolled the donjon-keep about,
Until the valiant De Vienne
Stood forth the crowd before,
And calmly said, " So be it, then!
I wot ye have endured like men,
And man may ask no more.
A parley let the trumpet sound,
And I, without delay,
Will for all souls in Calais found
Make the best terms I may.

Edward, for bravery renowned,
To honour bravery is bound,
And yours who can gainsay?"

XIII.

Once more throughout that serried mass
A solemn silence reigned,
As they had heard a sentence pass
And not a wish obtained,
Then slowly to disperse began.
For the last time the walls to man
The soldier shouldered his partizan;
Merchant, mechanic, artizan,
Matron and maiden, weak and wan,
With heavy heart and downcast look,
Each to their cheerless dwelling took
Their melancholy way;
And soon in each deserted street,
Not e'en the sound of passing feet
Gave sign that it was day.
And yet the golden sun now rode
In splendour up the sky,
And land and sea beneath it glowed,
And sparkled joyously:

As though the heavens themselves declared
For England, marching by her side
In all their pageantry, and shared
Her triumph while they swelled her pride.

XIV.

Shrinking from light that seemed but sent
To gild the glory of the foe,
Gaultier his steps had slowly bent
To where, of lofty limes, a row
Spread out a canopy of green,
The ramparts and the town between.
Beneath their more congenial shade
He wandered to and fro, and sought
Vainly to summon to his aid
One sweet consolatory thought.
Of evil, a presentiment
Heavily on his spirit weighed—
Evil extreme and imminent,
Though nameless, formless, undisplayed.
He heard the distant trumpet sound,
And well its mournful purport knew;
But though more gloomily he frowned,
'Twas not because that note it blew.

Gall as it might the soldier's pride,
Cessation from that hopeless strife
Would to the lover give a bride;
Blanche de Bellebourne would be his wife!
Restored to him by some kind fate
When the last faintest hope was fled,
Would not such blessing compensate
For any woe he well could dread?
Why, while his heart that truth confessed,
Was it so fearfully oppressed?
What dark, inevitable ill
Its dreary shadow cast before?
He knew not; but he felt its chill
Curdle the blood at his heart's core!
Out from beneath the limes he strode
Into the heat and glare of day;
Shivering, while all around him glowed:
The shadow o'er him seemed to stay.
Homeward at length he took the road;
In meditation so profound,
He marked not, where across his way,
Upon the sun-lit strip of ground
A shadow visibly was thrown—
The shadow of a man alone.

XV.

Anigh it as the burgess came,
A stranger voice pronounced his name.
" Gaultier La Motte ! " " If him you seek,
He hears.   What would you with him ?—speak."
The stranger, who before him stood,
Over his brows had pulled his hood,
And muffled in a mantle dark
Little beside was left to mark,
Save lips compressed, which plainly told
Of purpose firm and spirit bold,
The upper slightly graced with hair;
The chin close shaven, smooth, and fair,
As though some youthful clerk he were ;
Sweet was his voice, yet stern withal ;
Of bearing proud, of stature tall ;
Whatever mote be his degree,
No common churl, I trow, was he.

XVI.

" Thou lovest Blanche de Bellebourne?" "Aye,
As mine own soul ! " was the reply.
"What means thy question ?   Know'st thou aught

With peril to her welfare fraught?
Speak!—and speak quickly! Life and sword
Are at her service!" At the word,
The stranger off his mantle threw,
And from his brow the hood withdrew.
The coat-hardie and silver wrest
Bespoke the household bard professed,
But that a sword hung at his side,
Weapon to minstrel sworn denied.
Upon its hilt his hand he laid,
And fiercely to the burgess said,
" Then draw thy sword, and guard thy life.
For words, the time is past:
On yonder sun, that sees our strife,
One of us looks his last."

XVII.

Upon him Gaultier fixed his eyes,
With less of anger than surprise.
A smile across his features strayed,
Which pity blent with scorn displayed.
" What desperate wretch his fate thus braves?
Gaultier la Motte draws not his blade,
Because a nameless madman raves!

Go, fetch thy gittern, minstrel! Play
On that, and not on me!
Such dainty troubadour to slay
Would grievous pity be."

XVIII.

The scornful smile his foe return'd,
Though his blue eyes with fury burn'd.
" Good, Master Citizen," he cried,
" Would'st know by whom thou art defied,
Look on this scroll, and tell me then
If thou canst read the writing fair—
Deemest thou Guillaume de Brienne,
Viscount de Meaux, unworthy heir
Of Raoul, Count de Guines, may claim
To cross swords with one known to fame
So widely as Gaultier la Motte,
Burgess of Calais ? " At the name
Of Raoul, staggering back as smote
By lightning, Gaultier pale became
As death, the while his eyes shot flame,
And with contending passions high
His broad chest heaved convulsively.

XIX.

Suppressing, with an effort strong,
The tumult all his frame that shook,
The parchment from Guillaume he took,
And ran his eager glance along
The lines, which seemed his sight to blast,
Then stood, irresolute, aghast.
Meanwhile his rival, who that look
Misconstrued, and but ill could brook
Of vengeance the delay,
Continued, grinding through his teeth
The words, for wrath he scarce could speak,—
" I will not do thee so much wrong,
As think that name thine arm unnerves,
And drives the colour from thy cheek,
Because thy scorn no longer serves
To keep thy weapon in its sheath;
But rather I would say,
It is thy conscience, burgess, wakes,
And of thee now a craven makes;
For thou hast filched away
A treasure from me, in the love
Of Blanche de Bellebourne, far above

All price the world could pay!
Draw then, La Motte! or by St. Paul,
On whom my sires were wont to call,
Thy head shall like a felon's fall,
For grace ere thou canst pray."

XX.

Gaultier, his fearful struggle o'er,
And master of himself once more,
Stood pale, but calm his foe before.
All now at length he knew;
Nor moved he foot, nor raised he hand,
As in the sun-light flashed the brand
His furious rival drew;
But solemn as a passing bell
The answer from his lips that fell,
That charge and challenge to.
" If thou be what these lines declare—
And too strong signs of truth they bear—
Safely La Motte thou may'st defy;
By hand of mine thou shalt not die.
Strike, if thou wilt. Thy vengeful steel
No deeper wound my heart can deal;
For though the wrong my mother done

Should turn it into stone, I feel
I cannot slay my father's son."

XXI.

The hot blood rushed to Guillaume's brow.
" *Thy* father's son!—my brother! Thou?
Villain! the falsehood disavow,
Or at my feet thy corpse shall roll,
With the base lie upon thy soul!"
Unmoved by insult or by threat,
The honest eyes of Gaultier met
His fiery glance; so full of woe,
He shudder'd, as in accents low
The burgess said:—" The child of shame,
I challenge not a brother's name;
But of thy blood the proudest part
Now courses through this throbbing heart."
" Proof! Give me proof!" his hearer gasped.
And Gaultier's arm he wildly grasped.
Who answered, " Proof? Too well the tale
Is known in Surques' sequestered vale. (¹)
Still is the hapless fate of Claire
Whispered as warning to maidens there!"

XXII.

To hide the tears he did not seek,
That freely flowed adown his cheek,
As in a tone which to the wail
Of autumn wind at close of day
Might likened be, but that 'twould fail
Its depth of feeling to convey,
The story, sad as it is old,
How woman trusts, and man betrays, he told.

XXIII.

" Oh, she was fair! The lily not more fair
She wove at summer evenings in her hair;
But thus 'tis ever on the choicest flower
Fastens the worm, to sully and devour!
Thy father came, saw, loved, was loved again.
Wooed as none else had wooed—nor wooed in vain;
Left, as none else could leave, with human breast!—
Ask of the cross, that marks her grave, the rest!"

XXIV.

He pointed to a low white wall,
Beyond the row of lime trees tall.

It ran irregularly round
A small and humble burial-ground.
Therein, a little grassy mound
He often knelt beside,
And in that solemn solitude,
With pious tears the turf bedewed,
And clasped and kissed the cross of wood
Which briefly testified,
" Ci-gît Claire, dit ' La Belle aux Lys.'
Dieu de son alme ayez merci."
Who, that had known her history,
" Amen ! " had not replied ?

XXV.

At Guillaume's feet the scroll he cast,
As slowly, silently, he passed
Upon his homeward way,
Leaving his late infuriate foe
O'erwhelmed in wonderment and woe
Too deep to bid him stay.
Crushed by the unexpected blow
Which laid his hopes for ever low,
Even revenge he must forego:
A higher vengeance, sure, although

To man it seemeth sometimes slow,
Had fallen on him to-day.
A jealous God upon his head
His father's sin had visited.
" Vengeance," the Lord of hosts hath said,
" Is mine !—I will repay ! "

XXVI.

No marvel now—the terror shown
By Blanche, when first with joy and pride
He made his noble lineage known
To her, his brother's promised bride !
She saw the bar between them thrown,
Broken—it might be, blood-bedyed,
And felt as if on her alone
Would rest the guilt of fratricide !
The truth, which trembled on her tongue,
His frenzy would not hear;
The agony her heart that wrung,
And out of purest love had sprung,
He traced to selfish fear—
The shrinking of a soul forsworn,
As from its sin the veil was torn.
How he had wrong'd her now he knew,

And deeper shame on him it threw,
Such love to have belied.
He owned the retribution just,
His pride he trampled in the dust,
Each baser passion from him thrust,
And like to silver tried
Thrice in the fire, from out the flame,
Which but consumes the dross, he came
Chastened and purified.

XXVII.

Meantime, beyond the palisade
That formed the foremost barricade
Upon the city's southern side,
With barbicans well fortified,
Sir Walter Manny conference grave
Held with Sir John de Vienne, brave,
And 'twixt the town and camp
Herald and pursuivant to and fro
Busily were seen to go,
Till of their steeds the tramp
Seemed echoed by the hearts of all
Who watched them from the outer wall,
So fast, so loudly, did they beat

Alternately with hope and fear,
Amid a silence so complete
That each pulsation they might hear.

XXVIII.

The parley ended, they perceive
Sir Walter take his courteous leave
Of the old war-worn chief,
Who, through the wicket slowly now
Returning, bears upon his brow
A cloud so dark with grief,
The bravest of the burgher guard
Who keep within it watch and ward
Wot that the terms must needs be hard,
Almost beyond belief,
To shroud it in so deep a gloom,
And yearn, yet dread, to know their doom.

XXIX.

Know it they must, and quickly too;
Brief time have they in which to do
The task by Edward set.
Hurriedly in the old Town Hall,
Obedient to De Vienne's call,

The notables have met.
As it were in some hideous dream,
The awful words to hear, they seem.
Six of their worthiest,
Ere noon, in Calais must be found,
All born within the city's bound,
Who, with vile ropes their necks around,
To England's king, upon their knees,
Will humbly tender up the keys,
And dying for the rest,
With their brave blood wash out the crime
Of being liege men good and true
An undeserving monarch to,
By a devotion so sublime,
That of the tale in later time
The truth men may contest ! (')

XXX.

While pale and speechless with despair
Each gazed upon his neighbour there,
Up rose old Eustache de St. Pierre.
" My friends," he cried, " great pity 'twere,
And on our town a stain,
That hundreds should by fire and sword,

By headsman's axe or hangman's cord,
Or e'en by lingering famine fall,
When six have power to ransom all !
What life may yet remain
In these old veins I blush to give,
So brief a time I have to live ;
But still I count for one, and save
A better from an early grave."

XXXI.

" A better never breathed, St. Pierre ! "
Shouted his ancient friend, Jean d'Aire ;
" And though unworthy I
A fate so glorious to share,
Like thee to live hath been my pray'r,
'Tis now, like thee, to die ! "
While stifled sobs and blessings loud
Marked the emotion of the crowd,
Two brothers, wealthy merchants, named
Jacques and Pierre Wissant, rose and claimed
To lay their lives and fortunes down
For love of their dear native town.
A fifth, who begged it as a boon,
Was to the number added soon.

But up the fatal list to fill
One martyr's name was wanting still.

XXXII.

The day wore on, the hour drew nigh;
Stern Edward waited the reply.
Suddenly stept into the hall
A youthful stranger, fair and tall,
And in a voice so sweet and clear,
It rang like music in the ear,
Thus to the Governor he spake:
" I pray you, for our Lady's sake,
To suffer me the sixth to make.
Although to all men here unknown,
Calais a son in me must own.
Within her walls I first saw light,
As will this scroll attest;
And challenge, as my proud birthright,
To die beside her best."
The parchment, to support his claim,
He proffered to the veteran knight,
Whose brows with wonder arched became.
He gazed upon that face so bright,
That form all full of life and might,

Then read and gazed again;
And muttering, " By my holy dame!
I covet of that boy the fame ! "
He added to the list the name
Of " Guillaume de Brienne."

NOTES TO CANTO III.

Page 91, line 6.

(¹) "*Noel!*"

Literally Christmas; but in France during the Middle Ages a popular shout of gratification.

Page 98, line 21.

(²) "*Bourbon, and Hainault, and Burgundy.*"

Eudes, Duke of Burgundy, the Duke of Bourbon, and the Lord John of Hainault, were leaders in the army of Philip de Valois that advanced from Amiens to Sangatte with the intention of relieving Calais.—*Froissart*, chap. 143.

Page 101, line 14.

(³) "*What tongue the deep despair can tell?*"

After the departure of the King of France with his army from the hill of Sangatte, the Calaisians saw clearly that all hopes of succour were at an end, which occasioned them so much sorrow and distress that the hardiest could scarcely support it. They entreated therefore most earnestly the Lord John de Vienne, their governor, to mount upon the battlements and make a sign that he wished to hold a parley.—*Froissart*, chap. 145.

Page 112, line 19.

(⁴) "*Surques' sequestered vale.*"

Surques is a village situated between Guines and Ardres, in a thickly wooded valley. It gave the title to a barony belonging to the ancient Comtes de Guisnes, called Val-en-Surques. Three turrets of the old castle were standing in 1833.

Page 118, line 16.

(⁵) "*The truth men may contest.*'

And it is contested. The story is told by Froissart alone, and the researches of modern historians have brought to light facts which raise serious doubts of its accuracy. It will nevertheless long remain a popular tradition, and for the purposes of fiction an available " base of operations."

CANTO THE FOURTH.

THE STRATAGEM.

CANTO THE FOURTH.

THE STRATAGEM.

I.

In the long narrow " Rue des Carmes,"
Which, stretching from the old " Place d'Armes,"
Ran southward to the holy pile
From which the street was named erewhile
The Convent of the Carmelites, (¹)
A Hostel stood, where thirsty wights
In happier times had mustered strong,
And plaudits loud and laughter long
At Jongleur's jest or Minstrel's song
Had shaken roof and wall.
But many a dreary month had passed
Since mirth had held its revel last
In that smoke-blackened hall.

Above the open portal strung
A withered bush still idly swung,
And on the wall might yet be traced
In letters partially effaced
The words, "Au petit Pelerin,
Arnould Dubois, Marchand de vin."

II.

Therein, at a huge oaken board
On tressels propped, that oft had groaned
Beneath the larder's savoury hoard,
A gloomy group the fate bemoaned
Of the doomed city. Seamen they
Who with Marrant and Mestriel
Had nobly laboured, night and day,
By timely aid the foes to quell
That raged within the walls.
More fearful far than those who lay
In wait without to seize their prey;
As at the foot of forest tree
The coiled-up serpent you may see
Lie motionless, its fluttering prize
Watching with cold and cruel eyes
Till from the branch it falls.

III.

Rough men, but honest as the sun
Whose livery on their brows they bore;
Fierce men, who desperate deeds had done
In fight and fray, on sea and shore;
But once the broil and battle o'er,
A foeman's hand would kindly clutch,
And with their horny fingers touch
A feeble child or suffering friend
Gently as ever lady fair
Smoothed down her darling's silken hair—
Tenderly as maiden bright
E'er bathed the brow of her wounded knight.

IV.

Over a jack of Brabant beer
And a black loaf—their only cheer—
They listened now with eager ear
To the strange tale their host
Had from a neighbour's lips heard fall,
Of what had passed in the Town Hall.
And that which moved them most
Was, that the Minstrel, Arnould said,

Whom they had captive with them brought
Had proof of noble lineage made,
And on that ground had death besought;
And how he, Arnould Dubois, knew
The tale was not more strange than true.
Little entreaty needed he
To tell them how he came to be
Of the main facts possessed.
And without further preface than
At one draught emptying his can,
His guests he thus addressed:—

THE HOST'S TALE.

V.

" 'Twas in the reign of Charles le Bel,
Oft have I heard my father tell,
And I, though then a child, can well
Remember that wild night.
'Twas Lammas eve—a gale had blown
All day with fury rarely known,
And victim to its might
A Flemish barque, for Wissant bound,
Off Cape Grisnez was sinking found

By fishermen from Ambleteuse,
Who into Calais brought the news,
Themselves in piteous plight.
Her crew, who to their boat had ta'en,
Toiled manfully the beach to gain,
Nor vainly seemed to strive,
When within bow-shot of the shore
A mountain billow swept them o'er,
And of some fifteen souls, but four
Were brought to land alive.
To wit, a lady and her son—
A child of tender age—
His nurse, and one—the only one—
Of that ship's equipage,
Who had with them the breakers braved,
And saving them himself had saved."

VI.

" The lady was a high-born dame,
And wife of one well known to fame,
Raoul, the second of that name,
Who Count of Eu and Guisnes became,
And Constable of France,
And in a tournament of late

At Paris, his untimely fate
Met from a luckless lance. (²)
To join her lord at Tournehem (³)
In evil hour the Countess came
From Bruges, whither she had been
Attending upon England's queen,
The beauteous Isabel (⁴),
Sister of our King Charles, and who
Was mother this third Edward to—
Ah! Long the day will Calais rue
On which his birth befel!—
But to my tale. Half dead with fright,
Fatigue, and cold, that dreadful night
The countess, son, and nurse, were brought
Into this hostel; and as morn
Its light upon it flung,
Beneath this very roof was born
Another son, whose life 'twas thought
Scarce promised to endure the day.
And far too dearly had been bought
At price of hers who passed away,
Ere even-song was sung."

VII.

" It was a sorry sight to see,
E'en for a thoughtless child like me,
That mother lying stark and pale,
Unconscious of her infant's wail.
And the poor boy who sobbed aloud,
Nor would believe her dead.
And the old faithful nurse, more bowed
By sorrow than the weight of years,
Who gloomily glared through her tears
At the low-whispering, curious crowd
That, as the tidings spread,
Cluster'd around the door, by chance
Or favour, to obtain a glance
Of the young countess in her shroud,
The babe—or e'en the bed."

VIII.

" But eagerly, full soon, I gazed,
As much delighted as amazed,
When forth the solemn convoi passed,
And the escutcheoned torches blazed ([5])
Around the hearse with plumage massed,

And all the pageantry of woe,
Which rank and wealth on death bestow.
I watched across the sandy plain
The progress of that funeral train
Towards the final resting-place
Of all De Brienne's noble race,
Till the last torch, like to a spark,
Had dwindled in the distance dark."

IX.

" And here my tale had found its close,
But that next morn all Calais through,
A rumour ran, though no one knew
From whence it came, or how it rose,
That of armed men, a lawless crew,
Had fallen upon that mournful train.
The scanty escort—scatter'd—slain.
Pillaged the litter wherein rode
The nurse with the poor children twain.
And who for better safety there
In the babe's cradle had bestow'd
The jewels of the countess. Rare
And costly gems I wot they were

As ever countess deck'd.
One emerald ring, I mind me well,
My father said contained a spell;
But what its power none could tell,
And I as little reck'd.
It was the colour and the size
That gave it value in my eyes;
For even as a child I ne'er
To such like idle tales gave ear."

X.

" Beshrew thee, man! On with thine own!"
A listener cried in fretful tone.
" Pause not to prate of ring or stone,
When,"—
   " Pardon, friend, I pray,"
Rejoin'd the host. " That emerald ring
Anon will on my story fling
Of light a wondrous ray.
Therefore meet note of it to make,
Ye must not blame me that I brake
From the straight course away.
But up the sever'd thread to take
No more will I delay."

THE HOST'S TALE—CONTINUED.

XI.

" Well, sirs, on that disastrous night,
  The nurse who fainted had with fright,
  Upon her sense returning, found
  The cradle empty on the ground,
  And by it, bleeding lay
  The elder boy—alone—not dead,
  But sorely wounded. All had fled
  Who could escape the fray ;
  And one by one in grief and dread
  Stole back as broke the day :
  But where or how the babe had sped,
  Not one of them could say.
  In vain as lighter still it grew,
  They searched the tangled forest through.
  Nor trace, nor track which to pursue
  Held out a hope found they."

XII.

" The wounded boy was far too weak,
  From loss of blood more words to speak,

Than just sufficed to indicate
Naught knew he of his brother's fate.
Stabbed by a ruffian as in vain
He struggled boldly to retain
His mother's gift,—the slender chain
Of Venice gold he wore,—
He saw the infant's swaddling clothes,
In hopes of further booty ripped
By the same blade, while yet it dripped
With his own blood,—and heard the oaths
The baffled villain swore
As neither gem nor coin he found.
Then all became confused around—
He saw and heard no more."

XIII.

" Thus much in course of time was learned
From those to Calais who returned
Their mournful duty done,
And the sad story for a while
Served winter evenings to beguile;
But further tidings none
E'er reached us of the missing child,
Which more or less absurd or wild

K

Conjecture left to run;
Till, as of many a tale beside,
The interest faded, drooped and died,
And e'en its memory was almost
In the next nine days' wonder lost."

XIV.

" Since then full twenty years and twain
Have Lammas tide brought round again,
And now at length we know
The sequel of this tragic tale,
Which rises like a spectre pale
Wonder to wake with woe.
The babe then spirited away
Returns a gallant youth to-day
His life for Calais down to lay
And help the bond of blood to pay—
Our ransom to the foe.
The proofs are these.—The woman—she
Whose son he deemed himself to be,
When dying called him to her side
A solemn secret to confide.
' 'Tis fitting I should tell thee now,'
Quoth she, ' No child of mine art thou,

My husband who had in Navarre
Been fighting in "the Bastards' war" (⁶)
Brought thee, an infant home.
Whose son thou wert he knew not well,
Or if he knew he would not tell,
Nor through what fortune it befell
That he by thee should come.
Darkly he hinted of a fray
In which a part he bore,
And of the price at which some day
The babe we might restore.
For that alone thy life he spared,
And of the plunder he had shared
Produced of pearls a string,
A chain of Venice gold, a pair
Of earrings formed of rubies rare,
And a large emerald ring,
On which some words we could descry,
But neither he could read nor I.'"

XV.

"' A wild life he had always led,
Of neither man nor God in dread,
And wildly came its close,

A week had scarcely passed before
In drunken brawl at tavern door
Felled to the earth, he never more
  Alive from it arose.
May Heaven to him more mercy show
Than he e'er granted man below.
Forced from my humble hut to roam,
I sought with thee my father's home,
Gave thee my father's name, " Guillaume,"
And made thee as my son be known.
To him and all—for of my own
No child had I, and thou alone
  Wast given to me to love.
All my long weary life-time through
  No real joy I ever knew
Save that from tending thee which grew,
For on my head methought it drew
  A blessing from above.' "

XVI.

" ' My husband diced the chain away
  An ancient tavern score to pay;
And one by one the jewels went
For food, for raiment, or for rent,

But still I kept the emerald ring
Which might the riddle read,
'Tis thine—and may it to thee bring
Good fortune in thy need.'——
That was the ring of which I spake
And pray'd ye note of it to take.
So far good hap to him it brought,
He through it found the friends he sought
Who knew the jewel well.—
Given to his mother it had been,
For service rendered to the Queen,
Our royal Isabel;
And at the English court he found
That brother who survived his wound,
And on his father's death became
Raoul the third of that proud name,
Now Count of Guisnes, and who
In battle 'neath the walls of Caen
A prisoner by the English ta'en,
In England captive to remain
Hath chosen hitherto. (⁷)
And now, my masters, ye have heard
All I can tell, and every word
As Holy Writ is true."

XVII.

As ceased the host, the deep-toned bell
Of the Town Hall began to toll
Solemnly, as it were, a knell
It rang out for a parting soul.
The seamen started up and strode
Away without a word,
No need to question what might bode
The heavy sound they heard,
On their brave hearts they felt it smite
With a chill sense of fear
They never knew in storm or fight,
Let danger take what form it might,
Or death stalk e'er so near.

XVIII.

They mingled with the mournful throng
That streamed the narrow street along,
And denser ev'ry moment grew
As nearer the Place d'Armes they drew,
Fast filling with a motley mass
Of citizens of every class,
Crowding to see the patriots pass

Forth, to their self-sought doom.
While of each tower and belfry round
The iron tongues began to sound,
And in their dismal concert drown'd
The Town Hall's signal boom.

XIX.

And lo! they come! That noble band
Of martyrs, with a smile as grand,
A step as firm, a mien as bold
As though the hateful halters rolled
Around their necks were chains of gold,
And that sad summons but a call
To festal board in friendly hall.
Awe-struck, the vast assemblage stood,
Bowed ev'ry head, doffed ev'ry hood,
None spake above their breath,
And many hands were clasped in prayer,
And heavy sobs heard here and there,
And rugged men and women fair
With brimful eyes seen ev'rywhere,
And faces pale as death.

XX.

Aloof—some paces from the press—
Gaultier la Motte stood motionless,
Almost unconscious of the scene,
Conflicting passions torn between.
A brother in his rival known,
The fatal light that now was thrown
On all which, hitherto so dark,
Yet left of hope a feeble spark—
So fiercely, suddenly had blazed,
Blinded, bewildered, all but crazed—
Irresolute—distraught—
Around the ramparts he had strayed,
And mighty efforts vainly made
To rally reason to his aid,
But will availed him naught.
For the first time his Spartan soul
He felt unable to control,
There seemed no aim—no end—no goal
To the wild race of thought.

XXI.

Avoiding all who might have stayed
To question him or comment made
Upon his speech or mien.
Still more of meeting Blanche, in fear
Ere to some course of action, clear
And straight his course was seen;
Of all that had, meanwhile, occurred
No whisper e'en had Gaultier heard,
And still absorbed he stood,
Nor asked nor wondered wherefore there
Silent and sad assembled were
All who in Calais yet had strength
To drag themselves a furlong's length—
A ghastly multitude!

XXII.

A shriek! A woman's shriek! A cry
So full of mental agony
It startled every stander-by,
And for an instant turned each eye
From the martyr band away,
To where an old man strove in vain

A fainting female to sustain,
Who, as relaxed his feeble hold,
Sank at his feet as white and cold
As the stones whereon she lay.

XXIII.

Not long—for that soul-harrowing scream
Roused even Gaultier from his trance,
Of every anguish in his dream
It seemed the mingled utterance.
Of whose rent heart it was the sound
Instinctively he felt,
And clearing at one mighty bound
The space between them, knelt
Beside her, gently raised and laid
Her head upon his breast. The maid,
As though his touch some sense conveyed
Of evil, shuddered—opened wide
Her eyes, with terror glaring—tried
In vain to rise, and strove to free
The hand he chafed in his—while he
Murmured some words—he knew not what—
That spoke of hope where hope was not!

XXIV.

She struggled up. "Off! Touch me not!"
She gasped, as from the arms that would
Have aided her she broke away
With force by fever lent. "His blood—
Thy brother's blood—is on my head!
For me he dies! Gaultier la Motte!
Thy brother's murd'ress wouldst thou wed!"
"What raves she of thy brother? Say!"
Sir Bardo asked of him who stood
Aghast, as following her glance,
His eye upon the tallest fell
Of those devoted sons of France,
And features known too late—too well!

XXV.

Again her shriek rang through the air,
"Guillaume! He goes to death! Despair!
Father, why stand you silent there?
Gaultier! Thy brother dies! Beware!
Lest judgment fall on thee!
Save him! There yet may be some way;
Stay him! A moment only stay

Or Blanche a maniac see!"
"Guillaume!" exclaimed her aged sire,
In wonder, not unmixed with ire,
"Thou canst not mean"—"Yes, father, he,
Guillaume! the page, the foundling boy!
I was his life, his only joy;
For love of me o'er land and sea
He sought the proofs might give him claim
To wed with one of wealth and name.
Out and alas! They're found, and I
Have made them but his claim to die!"

XXVI.

"Can there be truth in words so wild?"—
"Father! Forgive thy wretched child!
In secret to be his she vowed,
If sinful was that vow,
Behold the fearful punishment
Offended Heaven has on her sent,
To duty's stern behest she bowed
And broke that oath,"—she sobbed aloud—
"Her heart is breaking now!
Gaultier!"—she turned—but he was gone.
Whither? and wherefore? There were none

Amid the sympathising few
Who lingered still around her, knew.
As by some sudden impulse stirred,
Without a sign, without a word,
That hint his purpose might,
He plunged the passing crowd among,
And in the thickest of the throng
Was lost at once to sight.

XXVII.

Rapidly he had gained the gate
Through which to their too certain fate
The chosen six must pass.
Calm and collected once again
His purpose fix'd, his course now plain,
He tarried for the martyr-train
Amid the serried mass.
As it approach'd, from out the crowd
Gaultier advanced, and with a proud
Yet courteous action, raised his hand
To stay the progress of the band,
Then thus in accents clear and loud
Jean de Vienne addressed:—
"Sir, I would ask, within these walls

Is there such lack of gallant men
That Calais to her rescue calls
This self-styled Guillaume de Brienne?"
He in whose teeth this taunt was flung
Started as by a viper stung
And fiercely forward pressed.

XXVIII.

"I warn thee! Tempt me not too much!
If of my father's blood thou art,
Something should tell thee thou may'st touch
A chord would make a demon start!"
To him la Motte made no reply
But thus continued eagerly :—
"Noble and gentle, all who hear,
Know Gaultier la Motte full well!
His scorn of falsehood and of fear
It needeth not to tell.
I have done some service to Calais Town
For which a meed ye owe—
I have won in arms some small renown,
As ten good scars can show—
I pray you for that service done
To grant me one boon to-day,

And by that honour, in battle won
I will count it over-pay!"

XXIX.

"Name it!" from fifty voices burst!
Jean de Vienne's loudest and first.
" Your leave, apart from all, to speak
To this stranger, if he dare;
If he refuse, your pledge to seek
Another this fame to share."
" Dare!" and the hot blood Guillaume's cheek
And brow with crimson dyed.
" Sirs, ye may safely grant his boon!"
" So be it then," replied
The brave old knight. " But brief the time
That we can grant for parley. Soon
The dial's hand will point to noon;
And ere that fatal hour shall chime,
Sir Walter Manny at the gate
Will for our final answer wait."

XXX.

" Fear not, Sir Knight," the burgess said,
" Six victims there must be,

And I will answer with my head
They shall not lack through me."
The crowd his courteous sign obeyed
And for the rivals passage made;
And up an unfrequented road
That 'neath the ramparts lay,
Haughtily side by side they strode
Followed by curious eyes alone,
For such their faith in Gaultier's word
No soul to dog his footsteps stirred.
Behind an ancient cross of stone,
That stood beside the way,
They passed. Still of their figures tall
The shadows dark were seen to fall,
And glide along the convent wall;
For of the Carmelites, the bound
It formed of their fair garden ground:
'Anon, a cloud came o'er
The sun—the shadows vanished. Fast
The fleecy vapour flitted past
But on the wall the sunlight cast
Those shadows twain no more.

NOTES TO CANTO IV.

Page 127, line 5.

(¹) "*The Convent of the Carmelites.*"

This convent was situated at the end of the present Rue Royale, then from that circumstance called Rue des Carmes, and on the site whereon François de Those, President of Justice, in 1689 built the edifice which became subsequently Dessin's Hotel.—P. J. M. Collet. "Notice Historique du Calaisis," 8vo, Calais, 1833.

Page 132, line 2.

(²) "*Met from a luckless lance.*"

Raoul de Brienne, second Comte de Guines and Eu, Constable of France, was killed on the 18th of January, 1345, by accident, in a tournament at Paris, held in honour of the marriage of Philip, Duke of Orleans.

Page 132, line 3.

(³) "*To join her lord at Tournehem.*"

Tournehem, a village near Guines, in which a castle belonging in those days to the Counts de Guisnes, was in the course of demolition in 1838 when I visited the spot.

Page 132, line 7.

(⁴) "*The beauteous Isabel.*"

Sister of Charles VI., called le Bel, King of France, and Queen of Edward II. The old historian, John le Bel, says she was one of the

L

greatest beauties in the world. The object of her visit to Paris, and her leaving it for the Netherlands in 1326, is differently represented by the chroniclers.

Page 133, line 19.

(⁵) "*The escutcheoned torches blazed.*"

In the illuminations of this period the torches carried in funeral processions are usually depicted with 'scutcheons of arms affixed to them.

Page 139, line 2.

(⁶) "*The Bastards' War.*"

In 1326 several illegitimate sons of the principal nobility of Gascony took up arms, and in concert with the English attacked several cities and castles in the French dominions. This was called "La guerre des Batards."

Page 141, line 21.

(⁷) " *In England captive to remain
Hath chosen hitherto.*"

Raoul de Brienne, the third Count de Guines and Eu, Constable of France, was made prisoner by the English at the battle of Caen in 1346, and was taken to England, where he was detained in honourable captivity for four years, receiving such marks of affection from Edward III. and his Queen, that suspicions of his fidelity were aroused in the breast of his sovereign, King John, who, on the Count's return to Paris in 1350, had him arrested in the Hotel de Nesle, and three days afterwards beheaded in front of that building, without trial, in the presence of the Duke of Bourbon, the Count d'Armagnac, and some other noblemen. His lands were confiscated, the County of Eu given to Jean d'Artois, son of Robert, Count de Beaumont, and the County of Guines attached to the Crown.

CANTO THE FIFTH.

THE SURRENDER.

CANTO THE FIFTH.

THE SURRENDER.

I.

West of the ancient castle wall,
O'erhanging the deep moat,
A church there stood, whereunto all
Who ever went afloat,
Ere up an anchor they would heave,
Or let a shred of canvas fall,
Would reverently pass,
Upon their patron saint to call—
Holy St. Nicholas.
It had been once a chapel small,
Whom founded by, none now could tell;
Some said he was a Prince of France,
Philip, surnamed Hurepel,

Who built the castle, and perchance
The church of Notre Dame, as well. (¹)

II.

It mattered not to those who bowed
Before the altar fair,
Who had erected or endowed
The earlier house of prayer,
Nor who of wealth or rank or power,
Had added transept, apse, or tower,
Or screen of sculptured stone,
For the soul's health of dame or lord,
Some crowning mercy to record—
Or for some crime atone.
The groined roof, the pillared aisles,
The corbels quaint, the gleaming tiles
The solemn choir that paved,
Richly and cunningly bedight
With arms or badge of lord or knight,
Whose banner, borne through many a fight,
Down from the dusky vaulted height
Above their helmets waved—
The windows, with their pictured panes,
Through which the sunbeams pour,

Scattering all their glorious stains
Like jewels on the floor.

III.

All these the people daily saw
With more or less of pride and awe,
But with far deeper interest view'd
The waxen models coarse and rude
Of human hearts and hands and feet,
Portions of limbs, or limbs complete,
Grotesque and ghastly mass!
Mingled with tools of various trades—
Weapons, boats, anchors, sickles, spades,
Denoting craft or class,
Suspended round the sacred form
Of him who had in strife or storm,
In travel upon land or seas,
From death, disaster, or disease
Preserved his humble votaries—
Blessed St. Nicholas!
Of maiden, mariner and child
The Patron, powerful as mild.

IV.

Nor were there wanting costlier things,
Of rich and great the offerings:
Chalice and patten, monstrance, pix,
Bowls, beakers, massive candlesticks
Of silver and of gold;
Which glittered in the mellow light
Of the tall tapers, day and night.
Gifted with tongues, what tales some might
Of guilt and grief have told!
More dark, more deep, perchance, than could
The poorest toy of wax or wood
Which near them hung, unfold.

V.

Amongst the many marvels there,
Of goldsmith's work and sculpture rare,
Stood a small ship of silver-gilt,
Like a good Spanish galleon built—
A "Nef," as people called it then,
With mast and sails and streamers fair,
Forecastle, deck and poop,
Whereon were tiny armed men :

Some standing in a group,
As if in converse deep they were,
Some seated, drinking, or at dice;
The whole adorned with gems of price.

VI.

It was brave old Sir Bardo's gift,
Pursuant to a vow he made
When on him Death came swooping swift,
And hope was none from mortal aid.
Unhorsed and wounded as he lay,
His life-blood welling fast away,
Upon St. Nicholas aloud
He called, and to his altar vowed
A Nef of silver wrought,
If out of that tremendous strife
He came with liberty and life.
The boon was scarce besought,
When o'er the roar of battle round
A shout, which caused his heart to bound,
Of " Calais to the rescue!" rose ;
And through the hedge of circling foes
Bold Gaultier hewed his way.
The old man valiantly bestrode,

And carved for both a bloody road
Out of the fatal fray.
Alas! to that good deed he owed
All he endured to-day!

VII.

Before that holy altar now
The veteran kneels who made that vow,
And prostrate him anigh
She for whose sake alone he pray'd
God and St. Nicholas to aid,
In his extremity.
But where was he the Saint had sent,
Of Heaven the chosen instrument,
In answer to that prayer?
And where his brother? Long, long lost,
Restored—But oh! at what a cost
To think they scarce could dare.
All they had learned—or sire or maid—
Was that ere noon should strike
Tidings should be to them conveyed,
Of one or both, belike.
But they were strictly bound meanwhile
To wait within this sacred pile.

Such was the message Marrant bore
From Gaultier; but he would no more,
If more he knew, disclose;
To hearts so wrung by grief intense,
Adding the torture of suspense,
Well nigh the worst of woes!

VIII.

A hasty footstep in the street!
Their hearts to listen, cease to beat,
To rise they scarce have strength;
Within the porch a figure stands,
Advances, grasps their outstretched hands—
'Tis Gaultier, come at length!
Alone, pale, grave, but self-possessed.
His words in answer to
The questions quickly on him pressed
Were brief and vague and few.
" Guillaume is saved?"   " He may be soon."
" May be! You doubt?"   " 'Tis not yet noon."
" And thou?" the old man asked, " and thou?"
" Sir Knight, I hold thee to thy vow;
And, Blanche, if e'er again in life
We meet, remember, thou art mine!"

"I swear by every saint divine,
Save but Guillaume, I am thy wife,
Thy slave—to slay, to sell!"
"Hark!" he exclaim'd, as from the tower
Rang out the first stroke of the hour,
"Blanche! He *is* saved! Farewell!"

IX.

He darted forth, ere on the bell
A second time the hammer fell.
And the poor maiden's bosom through
A fearful thought as swiftly flew!
With a wild gesture of alarm
She clutched her feeble father's arm.
"Saved! He said saved! but how? How saved?
With honour? Oh! if not, be sure
He will not live! Too well I know
His noble soul. The death he craved
A thousand times he would endure
Rather than life and safety owe
To subterfuge—submission mean,
A broken pledge, a craven prayer—
His sense of honour is too keen,
A life of shame he could not bear.

No, no! The hideous riddle's read!
Guillaume is saved, for he is dead!"
E'en as she spake the twelfth and last
Deep note of noon around them rolled.
The fatal hour was fully past,
And yet the truth was left untold.
Oh! if the worst were only known!
Her reason tottered on its throne!

X.

What sound was that? As from the tomb
A voice she seemed to hear.
" The dead arise! The day of Doom,"
She gasped, " is surely near!
Father! Look yonder—through the gloom,
Beyond yon grating—see you not
A ghastly form appear?"
By terror rooted to the spot
She stood; again more clear
The voice was heard, the form was seen.
" Blanche!" "On my name it calls 'Tis he!
Guillaume, my love! He comes for me,
In death as true as life
Yes. To the grave I follow thee.

There none can thrust themselves between
Our hearts that knit by love have been—
No other call me wife!"

XI.

Guillaume! 'Twas he in very sooth!
La Motte had led the fiery youth
To his own dwelling, there to see
Some deeds that would disprove his claim
To bear of De Brienne the name.
Roused passion, wounded pride, had swept
All doubt or caution from a mind
In which no mean suspicion slept,
No fear could ever harbour find.
And lured, upon the specious plea
That in a vault the chest was kept
Which held the deeds, adown a flight
Of stairs, along a passage low,
Guided by Gaultier with a torch,
Which scarce the way sufficed to show,
He entered through a ruined porch
What seemed an ancient pillared hall,
With dripping roof and mouldering wall,
But o'er the threshold as he stept,

Out, suddenly, was dashed the light,
And the next moment Guillaume heard
The door behind him locked and barred,
And stood in darkness and alone,
A captive in some place unknown.

XII.

Astounded—motionless at first—
But swiftly on his senses burst
The fearful fact—Entombed! alive!
No hope of succour near!
No chance his shouts could e'er arrive
At friendly mortal's ear.
Wherefore had he been thus betrayed?
If but his death their hope,
Why snatch him from the headsman's blade?
Or worse—the hangman's rope?
Death had no power his soul to daunt,
That, well enough his brother knew.
The base-born brother, whose keen taunt
Was prelude this foul treason to.
His rival also—base of birth—
Of spirit still more base—

Who—who but he on all the earth
Would do him such disgrace?

XIII.

Disgrace—for such no doubt his aim—
'Twas not enough that he should die
With honour. No! His spotless fame
Must perish too! An artful lie
Would brand him as a recreant knave,
Who, shrinking from a glorious grave,
Had been unmasked and fled:
First having filched a noble name,
Then left a worthier to claim
To suffer in his stead.
The love of Blanche 'twould surely shake,
Scorn would the place of pity take,
And leave her free the vow to break
In Heaven registered.

XIV.

Clearly the motive now was seen:
Revenge, as terrible as mean,
La Motte had deeply planned!
Naught less could glut his jealous hate—

Naught less his thirst for vengeance sate—
His father's crime, his mother's fate,
His bride's disputed hand;
Of injuries the heavy debt
That on his spirit weighed,
By this one felon act was met
And ruthlessly repaid!

XV.

All this through his excited brain
As swift as lightning flashed,
As 'gainst the ponderous door in vain
Himself, again and yet again,
He desperately dashed.
Wildly about the ground he groped,
Seeking some loose or fallen stone,
Wherewith to batter at the lock.
His hand encountered what he hoped
To find, but dropped it with a groan.
As if designed all hope to mock,
It was a human skull, that told,
As from his shuddering grasp it rolled,
Of one whose miserable fate,

Victim of vengeance or of hate,
Full soon would be his own.

XVI.

As more accustomed to the gloom
His eyes, by slow degrees became,
Of what might be his living tomb,
Some faint idea he strove to frame.
Dungeon or vault or catacomb,
Of either it might bear the name:
Huge columns in the distance loom
Whereon the ribs of arches meet,
And a stone coffin here and there,—
A fractured one was at his feet.
No loop-hole, or for light or air,
Could he discern, yet although weak,
Some light there was, and on his cheek
The air he felt—a rent perchance
Might in the further depth be found.
Cautiously forward by the wall
With eager scrutinizing glance
He slowly felt his way
The group of massive columns round;
Till from above there seem'd to fall

A feeble glimmering ray
On some half-ruined steps that led
Up to a grated iron door,
Through which, as if in doubt and dread,
Peered the pale light of day.
At the same moment the faint tone
Of a deep bell came like a moan
Upon his startled ear.
" Noon ! " was his wild despairing cry ;
" My comrades march to death, and I
Foresworn stand helpless here ! "

XVII.

As up the broken steps he sprung,
And to the bars with frenzy clung,
The well-known voice of Blanche he heard—
Upon the form of Blanche he gazed—
And for an instant stood amazed.
" Blanche ! " was the solitary word
His lips at first had power to frame ;
Then as in turn she shriek'd his name,
He shouted " Blanche !—For mercy's sake
Speed to Sir John de Vienne !—Say
That I have foully been betrayed,

And pray him only to delay
His march until he send me aid
These bars to open or to break!"

XVIII.

Ere her bewildered senses well
The meaning of his words could seize,
Trusty Marrant and Mestriel
Enter'd the transept with the keys
Of the old Crypt—all that remain'd
Of the more ancient edifice,
And to which entrance could be gain'd
Through Gaultier's dwelling; whose device
Thereon had hurriedly been planned.
While Mestriel approach'd the grate
The prisoner to liberate,
Marrant within the maiden's hand
A tiny volume placed:
The vellum leaves much soiled and worn,
By Gaultier, aye about him borne:
A Livre d'heures, which once had been
His mother's. "God! what may this mean?"
She asked, for often had she seen
The little book, and a new dread

Possessed her as the lines she read
Upon the cover traced.
Few! but too full of meaning they—
" Gaultier la Motte commends him to
The Lady Blanche de Bellebourne. May
She love the living brother so
That for her sake he will forgive
The one who died that he might live."

XIX.

" Died!—Gaultier dead?"—she dropped the book,
And staggering strove to stay
Guillaume, who dared not on her look,
Nor heed of what she uttered took,
But wildly rushed away.
Strength to pursue him she had none,
She stood as she had been of stone,
And fixed her wistful eyes upon
Those seamen twain, and at a glance
In each dejected countenance
An answer to her question read.
" Take me to him." 'Twas all she said—
The voice was calm and low—
But there was something in the tone

So piteous!—hardened as those men
Had been, from childhood upwards grown
In scenes of strife and woe,
Their cheeks with kindly dew were damp,
As huskily they answered then—
" Gaultier is in the English camp
In lieu of Guillaume de Brienne."

XX.

In the English camp that day,
High the feasting, great the glee :
King Edward's wooden town was gay
With garlands, flags, and tapestry!
'Tis noon. In more than wonted state
The sovereign banquets there.
The tables groan beneath the weight
Of massive gold and silver plate,
And piles of viands rare,
So profusely furnishéd,
Earth and ocean you might deem
Had been despoiled the board to spread—
Sturgeon, lamprey, pike, and bream ;
Haunch of buck, and head of boar.
Savoury pasty, mighty chine,

Cygnet, capon, quail, and more
Esteemed than all the rest,
The peacock, in his hackle fine,
With gilded beak and crest :
If ye may credit minstrel's word,
" Food for lover ; " " meat for lord ; " ([2])
Of dainty cates and sweets a store
Fair dame and demoiselle to please ;
Set forth with curious subtleties,
Leopards and eagles crown'd.
Out of golden cups they drain
Wines of Gascony and Spain,
Cyprus, Sicily, Almaine,
While to the trumpets sound
After every course they pass
The richly-spiced ypocras
In jewelled hanaps round.

XXI.

Now, turn ye from this revel vain,
Its fearful contrast to survey.
Look on the wretched, haggard train
That hither wends its woeful way.

The scraps beneath yon table cast,
Had been to them a rare repast—
The leader, like a spectre pale,
Upon a ghastly steed; (³)
The flesh of both combined would fail
One hungry kite to feed.
The men-at-arms who trail their spears
Dejectedly on either flank—
Poor skeletons! One almost hears
Their bones within their armour clank.
The magnates of the render'd town,
Greffier and echevin and mayor,
But for furred robe and ample gown
Their forms the crows might scare.
But mark the six, the march who close,
Bareheaded and barefooted all.
Compare their lot, with that of those
Who keep hard by high festival.
What awaits them?—For banquet board
The scaffold draped with sable serge;
For glittering plate, the headman's sword;
For minstrel's lay, a doleful dirge;
For jocund harp, the muffled drum;
For spicy wine—the bitter cup

Of death, which to the dregs they come
Freely to drink for others up;
And yet alone of all that band
Their looks are bright, their bearing grand !
Let England boast her triumph nigh,
Theirs is the greatest victory !—

XXII.

While yet within the royal tent
Reign'd minstrelsy and merriment,
A deep and dull funereal roll
Like far-off thunder rumbled round,
Mingling its melancholy sound
With harper's song, and jester's droll.
The laugh was checked,
The lay unrecked,
The wine untasted passed,
And every eye
Was anxiously
Towards the entrance cast.
The velvet curtains back were thrown,
And through the gay and courtly ring
The mayor and citizens alone
Advanced and knelt before the king.

At his feet the keys they laid,
Thus, a burgess to him said:

XXIII.

"King of England, on our knees
We tender thee our city's keys,
If by monarch crown'd of right
Loyalty is crime esteemed,
If by a renowned knight
Brave defence a sin be deemed,
Knight and monarch, then let fall
Thy sentence upon us for all."

XXIV.

The voice, the face, familiar seemed,
And as the light of memory gleamed
Upon the moody monarch's mind,
His brow assumed a sterner frown,
As on the speaker he looked down
With anger and surprise combined.
"Hah! my bold burgess!—art of death
So fond, forsooth, that at our hands
Thou crav'st it twice?—Waste not thy breath.
Such boon thine insolence demands,

And churlish twere to say thee no.
Thou hast it, sir.   The headsman ! ho !"

XXV.

A murmur of compassion deep
Throughout that proud assembly ran,
And women fair were fain to weep,
And gallant knights to frown began,
But ventured none remonstrance save
Sir Walter Manny, kind as brave.
" Good sir," quoth he, " some mercy show ; (4)
The loyalty thy subjects owe
To thee for these should plead,
Allegiance others may hold light,
Nor care 'gainst fearful odds to fight
If such be deemed the meed."

XXVI.

Fire shot from Edward's eagle eye,
And curled his lip contemptuously.
" Mercy !   To chapmen who could dare
Arms against belted knights to bear,
And by resistance rash and vain
England of blood and treasure drain ?"

With his hand he made a sign.
Far too well could all divine
Its import dread—yet strange to tell,
Those upon whom the sentence fell
Alone no fear betrayed.
Up from their knees they calmly rose,
And saw unmoved around them close
The archers, who obeyed
That signal, and took order there
To march them to the market square
In that quaint town of wood,
Where, waiting with his weapon bare,
The headsman grimly stood.

XXVII.

At the same moment, dashing past
The startled sentinels, who cast
Their spears across his course to stay,
But which like straws aside he thrust,
A seeming madman forced his way
Wildly the royal daïs to.
"Hold! by the saints in whom ye trust!"
He shouted, as himself he threw
At Edward's feet, who, all amazed,

Upon the rash intruder gazed,
Yet with proud gesture checked
The knights and squires that forward flew,
And hastily their weapons drew
Their sovereign to protect.
" What villain dares——" " No villain, king !
For justice to thy knees I cling.
I, Guillaume, Viscount de Brienne,
Beg at thy feet a brother's grace,
Who, 'mid these self-devoted men,
With kindly fraud usurped my place ! "

XXVIII.

Of that sweet voice, the music rare,
Which neither anguish nor despair
Could of its magic power divest,
Its wonted charm on all imprest,
And touched in many a bosom fair
Of thought a tender string.
It needed not the locks of gold
That down his shoulders wildly rolled
To tell them that the pleader bold
Was " William with the Ring."

But the strange words his lips let fall
Were mysteries to each and all.

XXIX.

In Edward's court the queen alone
Of Guillaume had the secret known,
And thence the favour to him shown,
And place her person near.
To her the king an instant turned,
In few brief words the truth he learned,
And whence the likeness each discerned
In Gaultier now was clear.
But still the monarch's fury burned
Against the burgess who had spurned
His largess and his might defied.
Gloomily De Brienne he eyed.
" Foolhardy youth—begone, or share
Thy brother's fate." " Oh, king, beware!
Such blood as his to heaven will cry
For vengeance! Nay, I came to die.
And if thou art the noble knight
That Europe holds thee—do me right,
Nor let him rob me of my lot!"
" Sir king, I charge thee heed him not!"

Hastily here broke in La Motte.
"It is my glory thus to die,
Then curse not me with clemency."

XXX.

The monarch's passion mounted high;
With flushing cheek and flashing eye
Again he turned him to the queen,
Who with the rest in wonder mute
Had listened to the strange dispute
The rival brothers twain between,
And, with a woman's instinct keen,
Saw that some stake more dear than life
Was play'd for in that generous strife,
And felt with all a woman's heart
That love must own the larger part.
"Now by our Lady of Walsinghame!
Stark frenzy this! How sayst thou, dame?
Is this some antic our feast to grace?
Or are we bearded in pride of place?
Dearly their crime shall they abie,
Madmen or mummers, all shall die!"

XXXI.

Then up from out her golden chair
Arose that royal lady fair
And knelt the king before,
The while adown her cheeks like rain
The tears she could no more restrain
Full fast began to pour.
"Dear lord and gentle sir," she said, (')
At Nevil's Cross, by God His aid,
Of the wild Scots I foiled the raid,
And of their king a captive made.
Sith then across the sea,
By love still more than duty led
At peril to myself I sped,
And never till this moment dread
Have begged a boon of thee.
Now for our blessed Lady's sake,
And by thy love for me,
Sweet husband, grant the prayer I make
Upon my bended knee.
Oh think what chivalry would say
Should Edward thus give passion sway,
And with unworthy vengeance stain

The laurels plucked from Cressy's plain?
Mercy is the brightest gem
In a monarch's diadem,
On thy royal chaplet there
Shineth not a pearl so fair—
Oh let its lustre give thy name
A glory passing Cressy's fame."

XXXII.

The King, his teeth together set,
The prayer in silence heard;
The hot blood of Plantagenet
Was powerfully stirr'd.
The men of Calais he hated sore, (*)
They had grievously gall'd his pride,
For twelve long months on that sandy shore
They had forced him to abide.
And now that the weary siege was o'er,
So haughtily themselves they bore,
E'en with the scaffold their eyes before,
Their outrecuidance still the more
His fiery temper tried.
But Philippa was at his feet;

Could Philippa with tears entreat,
And be by him denied?

XXXIII.

Fierce was the contest for awhile,
But Love, which can the lion tame,
Was victor in the strife.
The cloudy forehead clear became,
And with a half reproachful smile
He raised his weeping wife.
" As thou wilt, sweetheart, let it be,
I give them, Philippa, to thee,
But frankly, by my fay!
Much as I love thee, dearest Queen,
I had as lief thou hadst not been
So near to us this day."
Boots it to say what hearty shout
Within the royal tent arose,
Or how 'twas echoed from without
As fast the tidings spread about
'Mid anxious friends and generous foes?
For certes, ye can wot it well,
And leave we Chroniclers to tell

What afterwards the town befell—
Our story hastens to its close.

XXXIV.

Amid the crowd that flock'd around
The liberated men,
A pale and trembling girl was found,
Alone, untended—but for whom
Soldier and citizen
Alike made reverently room,
For well by all of Calais there
The Lady with the raven hair
Was known and worshipped too, I ween,
So long had she to high and low,
In famine, fever, pain or woe
A ministering Angel been.
To meet her both the brothers flew,
And with her from the throng withdrew
Without a word. Too full for speech
Was the tumultuous heart of each.
Gaultier was the first who broke
That silence. Solemnly he spoke.

XXXV.

"Blanche, well thou know'st, in Cressy's fearful fray
It was my lot thy father's life to save,
And for that deed thy hand to me he gave:
'Tis mine! mine doubly by thine oath to-day.
Be witness, Heaven, thus I with it part—
Give it, dear SISTER, where thou gavest thy heart."

NOTES TO CANTO V.

Page 158, line 2.

(¹) *" The Church of Notre Dame as well."*

The two churches or chapels of Notre Dame and of St. Nicholas were supposed to have been built or restored by Philippe de France, surnamed Hurepel, who by his marriage with Mahaud, daughter of Renaud, Comte de Boulogne, A.D. 1216, succeeded to the county, and in 1224 surrounded Calais with walls, and in 1227 built the castle. Nothing positive has, however, been discovered as to their foundation, or that of the original edifices, but they were the only churches existing in Calais at the time of the siege. The chapel of St. Nicholas was situated at the west end of the town—" dans le lieu actuellement occupé par les fosses de la citadelle." After the siege a magnificent church was erected on its site, in which Richard II. was married to Isabella, daughter of Charles VI., by the Archbishop of Canterbury, November 3, 1396. This church was also pulled down in 1564 for the construction of further fortifications.—*P. J. M. Collet.*

Page 175, line 6.

(²) *" Food for lover, meat for lord."*

" Chez nos vieux Romanciers le Paon est qualifié du titre de 'Noble Oiseau,' et sa chair y est regardée comme 'la nourriture des amants' et comme 'la viande des Preux.' "—*Le Grand D'Aussy—Vie Privée des Français.*

Page 176, line 4.

(³) "*Upon a ghastly steed.*"

"The Lord John de Vienne then mounted a small hackeney, for it was with difficulty he could walk, and conducted them to the gate, ... which the Governor ordered to be opened, and then shut upon him and the six citizens, whom he led to the barriers."—*Froissart,* book I. chap. 145.

Page 179, line 9.

(⁴) "*Good sir,*" quoth he, "*some mercy show.*"

Sir Walter Manny, according to Froissart, had given his promise to Sir John de Vienne to do all in his power to save them, and had told the King, " You will set us a very bad example, for if you order us to go to any of your castles, we shall not obey you so cheerfully if you put these people to death, for they will retaliate upon us in a similar case."—*Ibid.*

Page 184, line 7.

(⁵) "*Dear lord and gentle sir,*" she said.

The Queen of England fell on her knees and with tears said, "Ah, gentle Sir, since I have crossed the sea with great danger to see you, I have never asked you one favour; now I humbly ask as a gift, for the sake of the Son of the blessed Mary, and for your love to me, that you will be merciful to these six men." The King looked at her for some time in silence, and then said, "Ah, Lady, I wish you had been anywhere else than here: you have entreated in such a manner that I cannot refuse you; I therefore give them to you to do as you please with them."—*Ibid.*

Page 185, line 12.

(⁶) *"The men of Calais he hated sore."*

"The King eyed them with angry looks (for he hated much the people of Calais for the great losses he had formerly suffered from them at sea)," and now had " by their obstinate defence cost him so many lives and so much money" that he was "mightily enraged."— *Ibid.*

FINIS.

BRADBURY, EVANS, AND CO., PRINTERS, WHITEFRIARS.

www.ingramcontent.com/pod-product-compliance
Lightning Source LLC
Chambersburg PA
CBHW032144160426
43197CB00008B/767